D0758309

SO SHALL YE REAP

SO SHALL YE REAP

Joan London and
Henry Anderson

THOMAS Y. CROWELL COMPANY
New York   Established 1834

Copyright © 1970 by Joan London and Henry Anderson

All rights reserved. Except for use in a review,
the reproduction or utilization of this work in
any form or by any electronic, mechanical, or
other means, now known or hereafter invented,
including xerography, photocopying, and record-
ing, and in any information storage and retrieval
system is forbidden without the written permission
of the publisher. Published simultaneously in
Canada by Fitzhenry & Whiteside Limited, Toronto.

Designed by Edwin H. Kaplin

Manufactured in the United States of America

L.C. Card 76–137823

ISBN 0–690–75365–9

1 2 3 4 5 6 7 8 9 10

331.89
L847s

To the memory of
Martin Luther King, Jr.,
and Robert F. Kennedy:
friends of the farm labor movement

WITHDRAWN

WITHDRAWN

MILLS COLLEGE
LIBRARY

Contents

PHOTOGRAPHS ON PAGES 61–76

Foreword

   This is the story of a social movement: the long effort of agricultural workers in California to organize themselves into associations, or unions, to improve their lives.

We believe the story is interesting in itself, and beyond itself. California's peasantry is not unique. The peasantry of much of the world is on the move, and so are many other kinds of people who feel that injustice is being done them. Industrialized Western democracies, however unintentionally, have set in motion a river of rising expectations. No one can gather up these waters and return them to their sources.

Some of the stirring is unorganized, but the world's aggrieved are increasingly turning to social movements: shared, organized visions which enlist strong loyalties, offer bold alternatives to established attitudes and power distributions, and hold out the prospect of very rapid change as social changes go. Whether one is sympathetic to this particular form of change or deplores it, anyone who wishes to understand contemporary history—and coming history—must understand social movements.

In our account of the farm labor movement, we do not pretend to a spurious, quasi-sociological objectivity, which is unattainable in such matters, and would be undesirable even if it were attainable, for it would vitiate the kind of understanding which is needed. Why does a movement arise in one place, and not in another where conditions are "worse"? How does a movement kindle the spirit of previously dispirited people? How does it sustain hope in the face of what would seem crushing reversals? Under what circumstances are men moved to think in unaccustomed ways, to break out of the straitjacket of social custom, to sacrifice their ease, their careers, everything? These are the big questions, and they cannot be answered satisfactorily by anyone who has not himself yielded profoundly to belief, looked deeply into his interior castle, and returned to tell about it.

Most of our story is told in terms of pioneers in the farm labor movement: men who departed from the comfortable highways of our social order and struck out in a new direction, hacking through the densest kinds of political and economic undergrowth, blazing trails which they believed would lead to greater equity for agricultural workers.

To the man on the trail, all abstract formulations are nonsense. If there is any distinguishing characteristic of the pioneers of social movements it is not that they have "charisma," whatever that may mean; it is not that they are agitators, or zealots, or any other psychological "type"; it is that they fall short of what they undertake, and are usually soon forgotten.

If it be true, as Vergniaud said, that revolutions devour their own children, it is even more true that social movements devour their own parents. Later generations, resting in Canaan, pass easy judgments: the pioneers did not reach the goal because they were too naïve, too impetuous, too doctrinaire, or flawed in some other way. From there, it is a short step to forgetting them altogether.

But even as the pioneers seem to fail, they succeed. By daring to challenge the reigning ways of looking at the world, the men on the trail who are ahead of their time reduce the monopoly of the old order over men's assumptions, which constitutes its great and subtle power. With the possible exception of Cesar Chavez, on whom the final evidence is not yet in, the biographical sketches in this volume are "profiles in failure," as history customarily calculates success and failure. So much the worse for history, and for us all.

Father Thomas McCullough, Fred Van Dyke, and Ernesto Galarza are no longer part of the farm labor movement, but if they had not dared the things they dared, the movement would not be what it is, Chavez would not have accomplished what he has accomplished, the total quotient of hope abroad in this country among disinherited persons would be reduced, and the quotient of despair increased by that much.

We take for granted that the reader is familiar, at least in a general way, with the conditions of migratory and seasonal farm laborers: problems of wages, insecurity, housing, health, child labor, education, and so forth. If the reader is not, many descriptive accounts are available. The emphasis here is on farm workers' collective responses to those conditions which the agricultural industry itself has sowed. Hence our title, *So Shall Ye Reap*.

The manuscript has been read in part or in its entirety by Ernesto Galarza, H. L. Mitchell, Arthur Brunwasser, Paul Taylor, and others. We appreciate and acknowledge their advice, but we have not always followed it. The responsibilities for factual statements and interpretations are ours alone.

Ernest Lowe and George Ballis placed at our disposal the fine collections of farm labor photographs they have built up through the years. Stephanie Healey, Willie Hansel, Linda Johnson, Clinton Dupree, Rosilane Greenbaum, Lois McCarty, and others assisted in various ways.

Portions of the manuscript originally appeared, in slightly different form, in *Farm Labor,* quarterly publication of Citizens for Farm Labor.

> *Joan London*
> Pleasant Hill, California
>
> *Henry Anderson*
> Berkeley, California
>
> May 21, 1970

After the manuscript was completed and galley proofs were being read, the long Delano grape strike and boycott, described in chapters 7 and 8, ended in victory for Cesar Chavez and the United Farm Workers Organizing Committee. Since then, Chavez and UFWOC have been attempting to organize lettuce workers in the Salinas Valley, in the face of antipicketing injunctions, jurisdictional raids by the Teamsters, and citizens' "right to work" committees. There will be further travail for the farm workers' movement, but we stand by the judgments in our concluding chapters and Afterword. Chavez and his union held out for five years against the grape industry, and prevailed; if necessary, they will hold out as long against the lettuce industry, and others. It looks as though Chavez's organizing methods have unlocked a door which can never be closed again. The line of progression from disputed social movement to accepted social institution seems now to lie ahead.

> *J.L., H.A.*
> September 8, 1970

FARM LABOR MAP OF CALIFORNIA

with major locations
mentioned in *So Shall Ye Reap*

Scale of Miles

0   50   100

SACRAMENTO
VALLEY

Peaches

Yuba City ● ●Wheatland

Grain

● Sacramento

Cherries

Asparagus ● Stockton

San Francisco ● ● Tracy

Tomatoes

SANTA CLARA ● San Jose
VALLEY

Apricots

Prunes *Cotton* ● Madera

Artichokes *Plums*

SALINAS VALLEY SAN JOAQUIN VALLEY

Olives Oranges

Strawberries ● Strathmore

Lettuce *Cotton* ● Delano

Grapes

Potatoes ● Arvin

Lemons

Oxnard ● ● Los Angeles *Grapes*

COACHELLA VALLEY

Vegetables

IMPERIAL VALLEY

El Centro ● *Cantaloupes*

SO SHALL YE REAP

1. Of Myths and Movements

California is a mother to myths and social movements. Her entire recorded history is studded with legends, superlatives, tall tales—some true, some hyperbolic, some unprovable. The very name, California, is said to derive from a sixteenth-century Spanish tale about an earthly paradise. The discovery of gold in 1848, and the subsequent Gold Rush, linked the state permanently with that precious metal and the fascination it holds for mankind. When oil strikes were later made in California, oil was called "black gold"; when fortunes were made in lettuce, it was dubbed "green gold."

California's power as a maker of myths and legends deepened as motion-picture companies chose to locate their studios near Los Angeles. "Hollywood, the dream factory," a cultural anthropologist called it. For nearly sixty years, through the shift from motion pictures to television, California has held her place as mythmaker to the nation and, indeed, to much of the world.

In the heartland of this fabled state is an industry larger than her motion pictures and television, her oil, her aerospace research and development: an industry which produces five times as much wealth in a single year as that taken out of the Mother Lode country during the entire Gold Rush. This industry is agriculture. California's agriculture has, over the past century, created its own myths and legends, as fanciful as any woven by the most romantic '49er, or the most imaginative movie mogul.

The mythology of California's growers begins with the claim that they are engaged in "farming" and are therefore entitled to the same privileges and protections as corn-hog farmers of the Midwest, or small peanut, cotton, and tobacco farmers of the Southeast.

In reality, California agriculture has never been characterized by farming in that sense. Most of its practitioners do not even like to be called farmers, with the bucolic overtones of the word. They call themselves "growers," "ranchers," or "agribusinessmen." The last term implies more than the application of large-scale business efficiency to the growing and harvesting of crops, a process described thirty years ago by Carey McWilliams in *Factories in the Field*. Through outright ownership, corporate understandings, interlocking directorates and the like, agribusiness is directly tied to transportation, finance, warehousing, food processing, wholesale and retail sales, and other ancillary industries.

The farm labor movement which has arisen to challenge the mythology of agribusiness nurtures some myths of its own, as movements always do. One of them is that there are no small or medium-sized farms in California at all. That is untrue. There are several. But they are finding it increasingly difficult to compete with the horizontally and vertically integrated corporations, the speculators who are only waiting to subdivide their land for housing, and the newest financial phenomenon, the "conglomerate." Conglomerates have given rise to a practice bizarre even by California standards: "farming" in which the "farmers" purposefully lose money, in order to reduce the taxes on their other corporate activities.

Projections from 1964 agricultural census data suggest that there are fewer than 50,000 commercial farms in California today—hardly more than a third as many as there were a generation ago. They average close to 700 acres in size, nearly twice the national average, and even this does not fairly indicate the difference between agribusiness and farming in the traditional sense. California agriculture is heavily irrigated, which makes it extraordinarily productive; this means, in turn, that land values are high and one must have a great deal of capital to enter or stay in the business. The average value of a California farm has quadrupled in the past fifteen years. At last report, it was close to $300,000, well over five times the national average.

But even such impressive California averages conceal as much as they reveal. A mere 7 percent of the state's farms—those of 1,000 acres and more—occupy 80 percent of all the arable land. The top 2.4 percent account for nearly 60 percent of the hired farm labor. These are the giants who call the tune to which everyone who would remain within the industry must dance. For all practical purposes, everyone must sell his products at the same prices at which the giants are willing to sell theirs.

The large operators maintain batteries of lawyers to force court tests when it pleases them. They lobby with matchless effect for and against state and federal legislation which affects their interests. They dominate many executive departments of government. They retain Madison Avenue firms to manipulate public attitudes toward them and their workers. But whenever it suits their purposes, the giants drop the term "agribusiness," wrap themselves in the raiment and rhetoric of simple "farmers," and go before legislators and the public as the exemplars of Jeffersonian democracy, the last living examples of the pioneering and yeomanry which made this nation great.

On the strength of this carefully cultivated myth, California's agri-businessmen have been granted privileges unparalleled in the American economy. They profit, on a Brobdingnagian scale, from all the programs and subsidies designed to benefit small farmers. The Land Grant College Act of 1862, for instance, was intended to give farm boys free training in the agricultural and mechanical sciences so that they could return to the land as better farmers. The University of California, created under this Act, has tended, rather, to support developments which drive small operators off the land. It spends millions of dollars perfecting agricultural machines so expensive they are useful mainly to large operators. For many years, county agents of the University's Agricultural Extension Service openly served as recruiters for the Farm Bureau Federation, consistently the most conservative organization in agriculture. The Farm Bureau had its state headquarters on the University's Berkeley campus.

The Agricultural Adjustment Act of 1933 was intended to shore up, through price supports and curbs on overproduction, the income of small farmers who were often cruelly buffeted in the marketplace. One of the principal commodities with which the Act is concerned is cotton. In California, there are no tenant farmers trying to eke out a livelihood on a cotton allotment of five or ten acres. Cotton empires are among the largest in the state. One California "farmer" received $4.37 million for *not* growing cotton on part of his holdings in 1969; another, $3.41 million.

In addition to benefits under such national farm programs, California growers enjoy some subsidies which are not generally available elsewhere. For practical purposes, the Reclamation Act of 1902 functions only in the arid West. Under this law, the federal government builds dams for flood control, electric power, and the storage of water which it delivers, during the dry season, through hundreds of miles of canals. Irrigation water is delivered to growers at a fifth to a third of its actual cost—but, according to the law, not to the enrichment of speculators, corporations, and conglomerates. The subsidy is supposedly available only to farms of 160 acres which are owner-occupied.

Even when the law is honored, the subsidy is considerable. In the lower end of the San Joaquin Valley, for instance, growers pay $3.50 per acre-foot for water which costs the government $14 per acre-foot to capture, store, and deliver through the Friant-Kern Canal. (An acre-foot is about 326,000 gallons: the amount necessary to cover an acre of land with exactly twelve inches of water.) Since agriculture in this part of the state requires about three acre-feet of water per year, the subsidy is over $30 per acre per year, or nearly $5,000 on 160 acres.

In addition, the farmer enjoys a windfall if he sells his holdings. Unwatered land in California, where virtually no rain falls between late April and early November, is worth only a few dollars an acre to perhaps $500 an acre at the most. Irrigated land fetches $1,000 to $2,000 an acre, depending on type of crop and fertility of soil. Availability of federally developed water enhances a farm's value, on the average, about $1,000 an acre, or over $150,000 on a 160-acre tract.

All this is within the intent of the law. Congress was of the opinion, and has repeatedly reaffirmed, that family farming is so desirable a way of life that its preservation through such subsidies is worth the cost. But Paul S. Taylor, professor emeritus of economics at the University of California, and probably the country's leading authority on the Reclamation Act, estimates that at least 900,000 acres of California farm land are receiving publicly developed water in violation of the "160-acre limitation."

The agency responsible for enforcement, the United States Department of the Interior, does not seriously enforce many key provisions of the Act—such as the requirement that recipients live on or "in the neighborhood of" their land—and often makes arbitrary administrative rulings which undermine the intention of the law. For example, the Department has ruled that a "family farm" may include multiples of 160 acres for spouses, sons, daughters, nephews, and other relatives. In a particularly breathtaking order, Secretary of the Interior Ray

Lyman Wilbur, in one of his last acts before leaving office in 1933, ruled that more than 400,000 acres of the Imperial Valley irrigation district, wholly dependent on Colorado River water, were to be excluded from the 160-acre limitation. When this ruling was reversed by Interior Secretary Stewart Udall, thirty years later, Udall was challenged in court by Imperial County growers, and the case promises to drag on for years—during all of which the growers will continue to receive the questionable subsidy which by now they regard as an unquestionable right.

The "illegal" irrigation subsidy in California approaches $30 million in the value of the water each year, and a billion dollars in the value of the land.

Enormous as such subsidies are, however, in the last analysis the largest government subsidy of all to California agribusiness has been a guarantee of plentiful, cheap labor. According to the agribusiness mythology, farm labor has been a matter strictly between employers and employees, as befits the "last stronghold of free enterprise." The truth is that government has persistently intervened in the farm labor market, at both state and national levels, and almost invariably on the side of growers.

Government has discriminated in favor of agricultural employers and against agricultural workers in practically all major social and labor legislation. Agriculture is exempt from the state-federal unemployment insurance system, which in California amounts to a subsidy of 3.0 percent of payroll, or about $20 million a year. Only a minority of agricultural workers are covered by Social Security, which is, in effect, a subsidy to employers consisting of 4.8 percent of the wages of those who are not covered. For thirty years, until 1967, agricultural workers were excluded from the Fair Labor Standards Act, with its keystone concept of a minimum wage. Even today, only about 35 percent of farm laborers are covered; their minimum is 25 cents an hour lower than that in other industries; they are still excluded from the overtime provisions of the Act; and enforcement is almost nonexistent.

More important than any of these, the California legislature and U.S. Congress have excluded agribusiness from all collective bargaining laws, such as the Wagner Act of 1935, which made possible the establishment of labor unions in other mass-production industries. At the present time, in California industries other than agriculture, union-negotiated wages and fringe benefits average more than $4.00 an hour. Wages in agriculture—there is little point in mentioning fringe benefits, since there are none—average only a little over one-third of that. The difference between wages as they are, and what they would be if they were competitive with other basic industries, may be thought of as a subsidy to agricultural employers (and to consumers, to the extent it is passed on in the form of lower food and fiber prices). It amounts to at least a billion dollars a year in California.

Finally, the government has uniquely succored California landowners for a full century by acquiescence—and, frequently, direct assistance—in opening up one pool after another of low-wage, semicaptive labor, usually foreign, pigmented, and non-English speaking: gang labor, without counterpart in any other industry, and, indeed, specifically denied to every other industry in the country during most of these hundred years, as contrary to the public interest.

The mythology has it that California's bonanza agricultural style is somehow rooted in the natural scheme of things, and that it was necessary to scour the world for a labor supply tailored to fit this peculiar type of "farming." A University of California agricultural economist, Varden Fuller, persuasively argues that the reverse was the case: a peculiar type of agriculture evolved to fit the kind of labor supply already at hand, and once a vested interest in large-scale, labor-intensive agriculture developed, it tended to rationalize and perpetuate itself.

California Indians were the state's first farm workers. When Spanish settlement began, they numbered perhaps 300,000. On the eve of the Gold Rush, disease and ill-treatment had reduced this number to about 100,000. Ten years later, through a studious application of the policy of the American frontier—"the only good Indian is a dead Indian"—scarcely 30,000 remained, of whom only about one-third were able-bodied workers. The great Spanish land-grants, which had by then been taken over by American speculators, and the even larger grants of public lands to the railroads, lay fallow for the most part. There were some olives and wine grapes, but agricultural production was essentially limited to cattle and wheat, rather than fruits and vegetables which require large amounts of hand labor.

Chinese did not come to California to do farm work originally, but they remained to do so, and probably shaped the course of events more profoundly than any other single group. When news of the discovery of gold reached China, she was torn by floods, droughts, famine, local insurrections, and the Opium War (1839–42) with Great Britain. Thousands of young men turned hopefully toward the "Land of the Golden Mountain." By the end of 1850, there were already an estimated 10,000 Chinese in California, and they continued to arrive even though their passage across the Pacific was a cruel one, and they were generally despised by the '49ers. Their fortunes in the gold camps were summed up in the still-current Americanism, "not a Chinaman's chance."

In the 1860's, the Central Pacific (now Southern Pacific) and Union Pacific railroads received a federal commission to build a transcontinental rail system. Working from the East, the Union Pacific used Irish laborers for the most part. Working from the West, the Central Pacific used Chinese coolies: some from the exhausted gold fields; others imported directly from Asia.

When the transcontinental link was completed in May, 1869, only a few thousand Chinese were kept for maintenance of the rail beds. Some 10,000 were abruptly disgorged into the California labor market. Most of them, knowing scarcely a word of English, and having been tenant farmers or farm laborers in China, turned to California's agriculture, offering their services through "head boys" who had some knowledge of English—forerunners of the farm labor contractors who have persisted to this day.

The availability of this large new labor supply, when combined with technological developments, worked a veritable revolution in agricultural patterns. Rail transportation to the East made it possible to ship perishable fruits, vegetables, melons, berries to the nation's major markets. At about this same time, irrigation techniques were also being developed, assisted in no small measure by the skills of the Chinese themselves, although the mythology of California agriculture did not allow growers to admit they had learned anything of value from their workers.

These several factors produced a shift from livestock and wheat to fruit and truck crops, in which greater profits could usually be made. Demands for labor mounted rapidly. Runaway sailors and other Americans were reluctant to work at the level set by coolie gangs. To growers, there seemed only one solution: they imported more coolies.

The number of Chinese in California was estimated, in 1882, at more than 130,000.

In that year, due principally to virulent agitation by urban labor unions, Congress suspended Chinese immigration. In 1885, the nation's first codified Immigration Act was passed. Among other things, it prohibited foreign contract labor, without exception. This prohibition remained on the statute books for sixty-seven years, during some fifty-five of which it was flouted wholesale in California agriculture.

Happily enough, from the growers' viewpoint, at almost exactly the same time the supply of Chinese labor was cut off, the Japanese government relaxed its long-standing ban on emigration. Workers from the rice paddies of Japan began to appear, first in the plantations of Hawaii, then in those of California. By 1910, the census enumerated over 40,000 Japanese in California—most of them young, single males working in agriculture. In fact, there were probably substantially more than that. California farm workers—particularly aliens—have almost always been underenumerated by official agencies.

Japanese were, if anything, even harder working and more efficient than the Chinese. The labor-intensive style of agriculture consolidated its dominance. Large new acreages went into hops, sugar beets, strawberries. Anti-Asiatic agitation, led by organized labor in its San Francisco stronghold, mounted against Japanese as it had against Chinese. Anti-Japanese sentiment was reinforced from an unexpected quarter. Growers turned against their former "model workers," as the Japanese first organized themselves into the equivalent of unions, and then committed the even more highly original sin of acquiring land and becoming farmers in their own right.

In 1907, a "Gentlemen's Agreement" was signed, under which Japan agreed to halt the emigration of laborers, and the United States agreed to halt discrimination against Japanese. Neither happened. California passed a series of "alien land laws" which were not ruled unconstitutional until many years later. Agitation over the "yellow peril" and "the rising tide of color" culminated, in 1924, in a new immigration act which was frankly exclusionary and racist. Asiatic immigration was, for practical purposes, ended.

Once again, world history seemed on the side of California's plantation-style agriculture. As growers began to consider Japanese "undesirable," another pool of foreign labor was opened.

For years, Mexican citizens had been passing into and out of California, casually. The 1900 census reported only about 8,000 in the state. Some worked in agriculture, but growers tended to think of them as "lazy" and "undependable" by comparison with their coolie-gang ideal. In 1910, a long-brewing revolution broke out in Mexico, and kept the country in turmoil throughout the rest of the decade. Tens of thousands of rural-dwellers and their families fled to California. Some observed the immigration formalities of the time; some did not. By 1920, the census reported nearly 100,000 Mexican nationals in the state. There were doubtless far more. Most were dependent on day labor in agriculture. Growers began to discern admirable qualities in Mexicans, which had somehow been overlooked before. They were eminently tractable; they did not make demands, organize, or aspire to land ownership.

With the exception of a period in the 1930's, Mexicans have provided the bulk of the farm labor in California for nearly sixty years. It is crucial, however, to distinguish between several basically different subgroups whose only common characteristic is Mexican ancestry. First-generation immigrants usually tend to be relatively compliant. Second- and third-generation Mexican-Americans usually expect to be treated as something better than peons. When this expectation is not met, they leave agriculture if at all possible. In order for growers to maintain the style of labor relations to which they have become accustomed, they must continually replenish their labor pool with recruits from Mexico who are unspoiled by normal American standards.

The new arrivals have come under various auspices. Thousands have come, and still do, as "wetbacks," in ignorance of or deliberate contravention of immigration laws. In some ways, wetbacks are peculiarly at the mercy of employers and labor contractors. In other ways, however, even wetbacks are freer than the second major class of Mexican farm workers: contract laborers, forced to work for whomever they are told, under terms set by growers unilaterally, and required to return to Mexico at the end of the contract.

Although contract labor was against public policy as enunciated by immigration law, California agriculture received special dispensation to use Mexican contract workers during World War I, and much more extensively during and after World War II. In the years between 1942 and 1964, they were known as "braceros" (literally, "arm-men"). The bracero program, operated by a grower-government alliance, came to dominate the farm labor market. At the peak, nearly 500,000 braceros were imported into the United States in a single year—nearly 100,000 into California alone.

After a long struggle, led by Father James Vizzard of the National Catholic Rural Life Conference, Arnold Mayer of the Meatcutters Union, and others, liberals thought they had killed Public Law 78, enabling legislation for the bracero system, as of December 31, 1964. But growers turned to a third major source of Mexican farm labor. The McCarran-Walter Immigration and Nationality Act, Public Law 414, passed in 1952 over the veto of President Harry S. Truman, contains provisions uniquely favorable to agricultural employers. Under the terms of this law, thousands of Mexicans have come into California, armed with letters (often fraudulent) guaranteeing employment in agriculture. Theoretically, they are supposed to remain in this country. Some do. But many do not; they leave their families in Mexico, and return there every winter. Since the level of living in Mexico is low, they can and do work for less than permanent residents of the United States.

This latest wave of Mexican immigrants is commonly known as "green carders," after the color of the identification card the workers are required to carry with them. They are supposed to report to the Immigration and Naturalization Service in January of each year, but the INS keeps no record of how many are employed in agriculture or any other occupation. In January, 1967, 354,000 Mexican citizens were officially reported to be in California, which lends credibility to the estimate that there are at least 65,000 green carders working as farm laborers.

In the early 1920's, Congressman John C. Box of Texas introduced a bill which would have applied the national "quota system" to immigration from the New World as well as the Old. Apprehensive that their almost unlimited labor reservoir in Mexico might be cut off, growers cast about for alternatives. In an inspired moment, someone thought of the Philippines. Filipino contract workers had all the ordinary advantages of Asiatic labor: they were young, male, unencumbered by families, tractable, willing to work long hours for low pay at onerous tasks in asparagus, lettuce, and other "stoop" crops. They had, in addition, the extraordinary advantage of coming from a United States possession: they were entitled to enter as a matter of right, and could not be deported. By 1930, California's increasingly polyglot farm labor force included about 30,000 Filipinos.

In 1935, the Philippine Independence Act conferred commonwealth status upon the Islands, and contained inducements for Filipinos to return to their homeland. Some did so, but a majority elected to remain, despite the liabilities of all farm workers, the special liabilities of the Depression years, and even the more special liabilities under which Filipinos labored. All the old anti-Asiatic animus was turned against them, and to the usual prejudices and violence were added wickedly unjust accusations of "sexual immorality."

Through it all, crews of lonely Filipino men survived. Although they made up only a fraction of the total farm labor force in California, they operated in key crops, and in a remarkably well-synchronized, highly productive fashion, which gave them an importance far beyond their numbers.

American citizens have always been part of the disorganized army of farm workers in California. They have been tolerated—and, on occasion, encouraged—on one condition: that they accept the wages and working conditions acceptable to foreign-born groups. The domestic farm workers with the longest history have been single male migrants. As early as the 1850's, some disappointed gold-seekers, lacking skills for urban jobs and lacking money to acquire land of their own, took to the road, following the harvests. They became known as "bindle stiffs"—an example of the rich slang of the farm labor movement. ("Bindle" means a bedding roll, often with a frying pan wrapped inside it, carried on the back.)

To this day, single male transients form part of the California farm labor force, but they are no longer "knights of the road" in the nineteenth-century style. They live in urban skid rows, and get a day's farm work now and then through a labor contractor at a primitive "shape-up."

When times were hard, families of Americans joined the single male migrants, working when and where they could. Growers were willing to hire women and children, so long as they did not expect to be paid as much as men and did not expect such luxuries as toilets and drinking water.

Beginning about 1934, history once more unfolded almost as though California growers had written the script. Political stability had returned to Mexico; economic depression had come to the United States. Many Mexican farm workers chose to go back to their ancestral homes; others were forcibly deported. Some American farm workers were also leaving, in favor of the cities where New Deal agencies were beginning to function. One could make more under a bare subsistence WPA (Works Progress Administration) allotment than by working full-time in agriculture. At a time when one-third of the able-bodied men in the country were out of work, California growers began crying about a "labor shortage."

As if in providential answer to these lamentations, several years of drought drove thousands of small farmers out of the "Dust Bowl" of Oklahoma, Arkansas, Missouri, and the Texas panhandle. Between 1935 and 1939, an estimated 140,000 persons, destitute, frantic for work, arrived in California. Together with their dependents who were too young or too old to work, they probably numbered nearly 300,000: the largest of all of California agriculture's repeated waves of disadvantaged people, pushed by adverse circumstances where they came from, pulled by the myths and legends of the Golden State.

Most Dust Bowl refugees were independent farmers who had never worked for wages, but now they had no alternative to day labor in agriculture. They could not meet residency requirements for social welfare, and in any event they were not looking for "relief." They were a proud people, who had never asked for charity and never worn any man's yoke. Now they found themselves in a waking nightmare, dealing with unfamiliar crops, hostile employers and government agencies, competing frantically with each other for jobs. In some harvests, there were five or even ten times as many workers as needed.

In 1940, the United States began to mobilize, under a lend-lease agreement with Great Britain. Many Dust Bowl refugees abandoned farm work for the better wages available in war industries. Many others went into the armed forces, and when the war was over, stayed in the cities. But some remained in farm work, or returned to it after the war. Their lives had always revolved around agriculture, and they liked the work despite the patterns it had assumed in California. As the years went by, there evolved, by trial and error, a cycle of jobs which paid better than the average, and afforded something approaching year-round employment. These jobs tended to be highly skilled, involving picking, pruning, or thinning fruit: "ladder work" rather than "row crop" work. The several thousand Dust Bowlers who remain are now middle-aged. They usually work as husband-and-wife teams. They often do not think of themselves as farm laborers at all; they call themselves "fruit tramps." To Mexicans, Filipinos, and others, they are often known as "Anglos"—short for Anglo-Saxons.

Many smaller segments have at one time or another gone into the crazy quilt of California farm labor. Between 1907 and 1910, some 10,000 men were imported from India, while the U.S. government, as usual, winked at the law forbidding alien contract labor. Some years later, a group was brought in from Arabia. Contract workers have been imported at various times from U.S. dependencies such as Guam and Puerto Rico. Hundreds of Basque sheepherders from the Pyrenees have been used, and still are.

During World War I, public schools were closed and children went into the fields on "crop holidays," under patriotic urging. Boy Scouts and youngsters from the YMCA worked beside inmates of juvenile detention homes; deaf-mutes from a state school in Berkeley were used. Women "did their bit to win the war" in a creation grandly known as the Women's Land Army. Prisoners were in some cases put to work in the fields.

During World War II, patriotism was again the first refuge of growers. They wrote into the Selective Service Act an exemption for agricultural workers, but they did not upgrade the employment they offered to make it competitive in any way with other occupationally deferred classes. The consequence was a predictable "labor shortage," which California growers attempted to fill with various exotic groups and amateurs, rather than with a body of professionals committed to the industry in the way riveters and welders were committed to California's shipyards. Under such slogans as "Food Will Win the War," thousands of school children, teachers, housewives, and businessmen turned out to help gather crops, not really caring how much, if anything, they were paid.

Some Jamaicans were shipped in at government expense. Growers found them "arrogant"—perhaps because of their British accent—so they were shipped out, again at government expense. American Indians were brought in from reservations, but they did not last long; they tended to work with less zeal than the semicaptive labor which was by now the standard against which growers were evaluating all labor.

Japanese, who had been forced into "internment camps" shortly after the attack on Pearl Harbor, were given the choice of sitting idly in the camps or doing farm work. A considerable number chose the latter. In one of the less pleasant ironies of this history, their own farms had been expropriated, with little or no compensation, by their competitors.

In 1944, the federal government began turning prisoners of war over to California growers: mostly Italian rather than German. It has always been a cornerstone of the agribusiness mythology that swarthy-skinned persons are ordained by nature to be better farm workers than persons with fair complexions.

Convicts from county jails and state prisons were added to the several thousand farm laborers literally working under armed guard. Although braceros did not work under armed guard, their condition was scarcely more free. They almost always had to pay bribes to obtain contracts. To pay these bribes, they usually went into debt. Mexican moneylenders do not look charitably on bad debts. Braceros had more than the incentive of hunger to make them serve out their contracts with U.S. masters.

The World War II bracero program was also distinguished by the fact that the federal government bore the responsibilities and costs of recruitment, transportation, feeding, housing, medical care, and general administration. In 1945, it cost U.S. taxpayers $21,615,767 to place about 50,000 braceros at the disposal of growers: an average of nearly $450 per bracero, and far more than the average Mexican worker was able to earn in wages.

In the years since World War II, California growers have experimented with a number of other forms of semicaptive labor. They have imported some Negroes from Mississippi. They have imported over a thousand contract workers from Japan, nominally as "trainees," under one of the McCarran-Walter Act's more intriguing loopholes. In 1967, Governor Ronald Reagan made convicts available to growers, until the California Labor Federation brought suit, and the state Supreme Court ruled the practice illegal. For several years, rural county welfare departments have been issuing "work or starve" edicts under which parents on relief have to do farm labor, on demand by growers, even though they are not able to make as much working in agriculture as the minimal budgets allowed under the Aid to Families with Dependent Children program.

Through recent recruitment efforts, as through all the efforts to meet California agriculture's labor needs for over a hundred years, certain guiding assumptions hold sway. It is and has always been assumed that the dominant pattern in agriculture must be large landholdings, with either an absentee owner or an owner whose function is to supervise the labor of others rather than to do the work himself. It has been assumed that the labor supply had to meet the criteria established, initially, by Chinese coolies: uncomplaining acceptance of low wages, long hours, hard work, poor housing and diet, fearful heat in the summer, cold in the winter. The labor supply had to meet an exacting quantitative requirement as well: it had always to be available precisely when and where demanded, in larger numbers than objectively required, so that growers might have a cushion against a possible hot spell with quick ripening of the crops, and so that they could take instant advantage of any jump in the market price.

It has always been taken for granted that growers are under no obligation to care for these large numbers of workers before the harvest begins or after it ends. It has always been assumed that no matter how closely California agriculture resembles an industry in every other respect, it should not be asked to meet the social obligations which apply by law to every other business in which some men make a profit from the labor of other men. It has been assumed that even if laws were passed, they could be ignored with impunity. Finally, and most fundamentally, it has been and is an article of faith to

California agriculture, beyond examination, that workers must have no voice in the terms of their employment: that the industry could not survive if such a heresy were ever permitted.

When American citizens did not readily present themselves for employment under these circumstances, growers felt there was a "labor shortage" which entitled them to go to the most impoverished ends of the earth, in violation of treaties and immigration laws if need be, to find workers who would accept the prevailing conditions. The ultimate extension of this self-validating mythos is the assumption that it is the proper responsibility of state and federal governments, rather than growers themselves, to round up workers to fill the "labor shortages."

Since free men have traditionally rejected the prevailing conditions, the "labor shortages" could, almost by definition, be filled only by persons under some kind of duress: hunger, ignorance of common American standards, linguistic and cultural and geographic isolation, and, in some cases, an actual threat of punishment. To suggest that California growers crave a return to involuntary servitude would be unfair, but it seems fair to say they have historically depended upon labor so disadvantaged it was willing to submit to a condition which might be called "semivoluntary servitude."

Despite government acquiescence in the growers' unique universe of assumptions, despite the language handicaps and other disabilities of immigrant groups, despite a curious sequence of historical events which rescued growers time after time, one group of California agricultural workers after another has gained sophistication, has raised its aspirations, has questioned the sanctity of the system. Some have left agriculture quietly and been replaced quietly. Some have remained, and have raised their voices in protest. These voices have sometimes been lonely, but they have sometimes been joined by clergymen, urban workers, and others in a cry so organized, so prolonged, and so insistent it can only be called a social movement.

California growers have conceived this movement as a plot to destroy them: the work of ill-informed do-gooders at best, or, more likely, of professional agitators and subversives. The truth is that social movements arise when there is a gap between a society's promise and its performance. If there is no such gap, "agitation" may possibly produce a fleeting intellectual fad, but it cannot generate a true movement. On the other hand, if there is a serious gap between promise and performance, a reform movement is sooner or later the result.

The first essential ingredient of the farm labor movement was provided by the high promise of a society which claimed to value personal dignity, justice, brotherhood, liberty, equal protection of all the laws. The second essential ingredient, the gap, was provided by the mythology of California agriculture. Growers are men, not monsters. At the individual level, they have as many kindly impulses as any other group—perhaps more than some. But on any broad question concerning farm labor, their mythology requires them to hold out intransigently against the values which society at large professes: against the concept of representation elections among their employees, for example.

Myths serve certain useful functions in the lives of men, but they are also dysfunctional in that they tend to be immobilizing. At a number of junctures, growers might have deflected the farm labor movement, or scattered it in confusion, by a strategic concession. At all times, agribusinessmen had available to them the most effective of all possible preventives of farm labor organizing: small-scale farming. In this system, to the extent that hired labor is used at all, a one-to-one relationship exists between the employer and his "hand." They are friends. The hired man may even marry the farmer's daughter. To such an employee, talk of collective bargaining makes no sense.

But strategic withdrawals by growers would have meant relinquishing a belief in this bogeyman or that, this illusion or that. And to shift from large-scale farming to small-scale would have meant relinquishing the most basic of all beliefs in California agriculture's ideology. Like most of the rest of us, California growers preferred to cling to their illusions intact. That was the sowing; they are reaping the result.

Growers themselves are the progenitors of the farm labor movement as surely as slaveholders sired the abolition movement, and coal and textile magnates sired the child labor movement. Every day, they continue, unintentionally, to fuel the movement in ways quite beyond the power of "bleeding hearts" or farm workers themselves. Not long ago, for instance, Allan Grant, president of the California Farm Bureau Federation, chairman of the state Board of Agriculture, and member of the University of California Board of Regents, publicly explained why he felt there is no valid basis for unionism in agriculture: "My Filipino boys can come to my back door any time they have a problem, and discuss it with me. . ."

It would be difficult to compress into one sentence a more vivid demonstration of why the myths of California growers make the farm labor movement not only valid but inevitable. Paternalism is not acceptable in a society such as this, and it grows more unacceptable to more people all the time.

The farm labor movement has its own countermyths. One is that conditions are particularly intolerable in California. If the comparison were with health and safety provisions, job security, and other conditions in nonagricultural industries, even the most hazardous, disagreeable, and unstable our economy has to offer—lumbering, longshoring, food processing, mining, and the like—the California farm labor movement's myth would be no myth. Conditions are atrocious. But if the comparison is with industrialized agriculture in other parts of the United States—in Louisiana, say, or even on Long Island—the myth cannot be sustained. Farm labor conditions in California are, in that perspective, unusually "good." In their public relations efforts, California growers try to make much of this fact. To Cesar Chavez and other organizers, they say, "Why don't you go to Texas or some place where things are really bad?" and they imply they will happily provide the one-way ticket.

A number of laws concerning field sanitation, farm labor contractors, pesticides, and so forth, have been enacted in California—usually over the bitter opposition of growers, and usually with little subsequent enforcement. But even if growers had enthusiastically supported these measures, and even if they were all impeccably enforced, to suppose that such ameliorations would nullify the thrust of the farm labor movement is basically to misread the nature of movements.

Social movements do not gain their greatest momentum when and where conditions are worst, but when and where things have improved just enough to enable people to see that change is possible, and to give them a heartier appetite for something more nearly approaching the whole of society's high promise.

2. Up from Anonymity

One of the most dehumanizing things which can be done to any person is to strip from him his name, to turn him into a cipher—a faceless member of a coolie labor gang, for instance—so that no one is aware of his individual existence during his life and no one remembers him after his death.

By a similar token, an indication of the maturity of a social movement, how seriously it is taken, and how close to success it may be, is the extent to which it rises from the mists of anonymity and begins yielding names of leaders, ideas, places, dates, victories—and, for that matter, defeats—which are identifiable and memorable. In these terms, the farm labor movement has grown greatly in stature and maturity during its life of approximately a century.

The first farm labor "organizer" in California was an Indian who whispered to another, at some Franciscan mission, "Let's run away to the hills tonight." The first farm labor "sympathizer" was some Franciscan friar who protested that it was not saving souls to put Indians into virtual peonage, laboring in the mission vineyards. There were such organizers and such outside supporters, but their names are irretrievably lost in the past.

Next came the Chinese. To survive in a strange land, and at the same time preserve continuity with their ancestral customs, they required some sort of self-organization. It assumed two basic forms. In the cities, protective associations known as "tongs" evolved, usually based on one of the great extended Chinese families, such as the house of Wong. A member of a tong who was mortally insulted could expect to be avenged by his brethren; and he could expect that after his death, his body would be returned to China. The California Bureau of Labor Statistics reported, in 1888, that "In case of a strike or boycott [the tongs] are fierce and determined in their action, making a bitter and prolonged fight." There is no evidence, however, that they functioned as trade unions to any significant extent in rural areas.

In agriculture, a labor contractor system emerged to bridge the chasm between growers who wished seasonal labor but spoke no Chinese and coolies who needed work but spoke no English. The system contained some potential for collective bargaining, but only approached this potential in the hands of the Japanese and Filipinos, decades later. Chinese crew leaders tended to function less and less as representatives of their workers and more and more as exploiters. When a contractor was paid a certain amount by the grower for each laborer he recruited, it was often an irresistible temptation to furnish more workers than necessary. From a labor surplus, a contractor could also profit by the fact that he was usually the concessionaire for water in the fields, room and board, and a variety of enterprises.

Labor historians record very few strikes by Chinese agricultural workers. In 1884, Chinese hop pickers at the Haggin Ranch in Kern County struck for higher wages. The grower attempted to replace the strikers with Southern Negroes, but found them to be "too inexperienced"—an early indication of the often overlooked truth that most farm work in California is highly skilled, and years may be required to gain real proficiency. In 1890, a group of Chinese fruit workers farther north in the San Joaquin Valley formed a small union and attempted to raise wages to $1.50 per day. Such isolated efforts were quite easily brushed aside by growers.

The principal factor operating against Chinese self-organization was probably neither the labor contractor system nor the opposition of growers, but the fact that most Chinese field hands had no intention of remaining in agriculture. Most wanted only to save a little money and move to the city to go into business for themselves. Perceptive farm labor organizers, over the generations, have learned the same lesson as other kinds of organizers: workers without a permanent attachment to their industry are usually not willing to make the kinds of sacrifices which are required in a serious challenge to the prerogatives of employers.

Throughout most of the 1890's, the California farm labor scene was relatively quiet. During much of the decade, depressed conditions in the general economy produced a labor surplus, including a surplus in agriculture. In the early 1900's, however, conditions improved and many workers from other ethnic groups left agriculture for the cities. Japanese remained, became dominant in various crop areas, and began to capitalize on the possibilities for collective action latent in their ethnically homogeneous crews, under leaders who considered their interests identical to those of the other crew members.

Japanese crews struck in apricots in Alameda County in 1902. This effort was broken when they were replaced by whites from nearby Oakland. Japanese struck again in Sutter County peaches in 1903, and won a wage increase from $1.25 a day to $1.40 when growers were unable to recruit strikebreakers in time.

During the remainder of the decade, many such actions were recorded. Japanese developed highly sophisticated techniques, including not only strikes at crucial times but slowdowns and blacklisting of obdurate employers. In some areas, such as the vineyards around Fresno, agreements between Japanese crews became so effective that the labor market approximated a closed shop. All this was done without ever using the word "union." The proceedings of the 1907 convention of the California Fruit Growers include this passage:

> The Japanese now coming in are a tricky and cunning lot, who break contracts and become quite independent. They are not organized into unions, but their clannishness seems to operate as a union would.

The history of the farm labor movement in California would be far different if the Japanese had remained to develop their forms of self-organization and collective action even further. But they did not aspire to remain in agriculture as wage workers. They became tenant farmers, and then full owners, and turned their organizing talents to bargaining with produce brokers. When California's Alien Land Law of 1914, other anti-Japanese legislation of later years, and finally the "internment" of World War II drove small Japanese farmers off the land, they did not return to their former status of day laborers. Those who could not re-establish themselves as independent farmers moved to "Little Tokyos" in Los Angeles and other cities.

In some respects, the Japanese achieved results in the first decade of the twentieth century which the farm labor movement has never matched since, even on occasions when professional organizers and substantial sums of money were poured into the effort. But they left no organizational descendants. And, today, not one of their leaders is remembered by name.

The American Federation of Labor was only three years old when, in 1889, its national convention first considered assistance to agricultural workers. Charters were issued in the 1890's to small unions of cowboys and sheep shearers. In 1901, the biennial convention explicitly called upon the AFL executive council to assign organizers to agriculture. Some greenhouse employees, gardeners, and a few farm workers were briefly organized into "federal unions"—that is, unaffiliated with any existing union but chartered directly by and responsible directly to the national AFL leadership.

In California, the state federation of labor and various local councils, such as the central body in Oakland, passed many resolutions in support of organizing farm workers, and on occasion put paid organizers into the field. In 1903, a Santa Clara County group was chartered as Fruit Workers Union No. 10770. A number of branches were established, and they managed to survive for several years. This union was unusually self-effacing in its demands, and not very successful even in achieving those, but it is noteworthy in at least one respect: the name of its president, "J. Ryan of San Jose," was considered sufficiently important to be recorded in the commercial press of that time. He was the first farm labor leader whose name has survived to the present day.

Both the state and national AFL lacked understanding of the magnitude and complexity of organizing workers in industrialized agriculture. The problem was compounded by the AFL's commitment to craft unionism, which was wildly inappropriate to an industry where a man might have to work in a dozen "crafts" or more to fill out a single season of employment. The problem was further compounded by racial attitudes. The AFL was virtually lily white, while most agricultural workers were nonwhite.

As time went by, it sometimes seemed that the AFL ventured into farm worker organizing only to thwart someone else who was already in the field: someone the AFL considered too "radical." The first such challenge was thrown down by the Industrial Workers of the World. Hoboes and bindle stiffs were drawn into the IWW as early as 1906. Their aimless drifting became more purposeful. Some "Wobbly" organizers were farm workers themselves, and when they articulated long-smoldering resentments, around the campfires at night, their fellow single male transients listened and understood.

The IWW's perspective was unabashedly revolutionary. Scoffing at the AFL slogan, "A fair day's wage for a fair day's work," the Wobblies cried, "Abolish the wage system!" The AFL's concept of tightly drawn craft-union lines evoked the contemptuous epithet, "The American Separation of Labor." Wobblies believed that the class struggle must continue until all workers were united into "One Big Union" and together owned all the fruits of their labor. Hoboes, who had no stake in the existing order, signed up—10,000 to 12,000 in California alone, according to one estimate. They were uncommonly effective in "job actions," since, having no family ties, they were not afraid of going to jail, and were free to move wherever needed. With their knowledge of freight-train schedules, they were often able to move faster than paying passengers.

Conditions on the Durst hop ranch near Wheatland, in August, 1913, were representative in many ways of harvest-time conditions in other crops and in other areas of the state. Ralph Durst had followed the common practice of advertising for more workers than he could possibly use. Nearly 3,000 persons arrived at the ranch: about twice as many as Durst needed, since his drying ovens could handle the output of only 1,500 pickers.

A bare hillside was the workers' campsite, piles of dirty straw their bedding. No provision was made for garbage disposal; nine shallow, doorless privies, none reserved for women and children, had to suffice for nearly 3,000 people. Dysentery became prevalent. Wells, all at some distance from the campsite and the hop fields, began going dry. The only way field workers could get a drink, in the temperatures which rose above 105 degrees, was to buy citric acid "lemonade" from Durst's cousin, at five cents a glass. Food had to be bought at Durst's commissary, where prices were high and quality low.

That year, the going rate for hop picking in the area was $1.00 a hundredweight, but Durst paid 90 cents. Pickers who stayed through the entire four or five weeks of the harvest were to receive the other ten cents per hundredweight as a parting "bonus." Dr. Carlton Parker, who conducted a subsequent investigation, estimated that Durst profited by as much as $100 a day in wage hold-backs forfeited by workers who left in disgust before the season was over.

Among the pickers were at least twenty-seven different nationalities and, also, at least thirty card-carrying Wobblies, including two especially articulate and experienced organizers, Herman Suhr and Blackie Ford. Suhr remained only a day or two, but Ford stayed to organize a camp "local." He had no difficulty mobilizing the angry hop pickers. At a general meeting, Sunday, August 3, they agreed on a few elementary demands: drinking water to be brought to the fields twice a day; one privy for every hundred people, with separate facilities for men and women; higher piece rates; and abolition of the "bonus" system. Blackie Ford was chosen to convey these demands to Durst. Durst's response was to strike Ford across the face with his gloves. Later, Durst explained that he had done this "facetiously," an adverb which has bemused labor historians ever since.

Another mass meeting was held the next day, in a place rented by the workers for their own use. Some wanted to strike. Others advocated deserting the ranch and informing potential replacements about the insufferable conditions. No decision was reached. The peaceable meeting was about to adjourn, and the pickers were singing a Wobbly song, "Mr. Block," when Durst, his personal lawyer who was also the county district attorney, the sheriff, and several armed deputies burst in. One of the deputies fired a shot "to quiet the mob." It was too much for the desperate farm workers. The Wheatland Riot began.

The district attorney, a sheriff's deputy, and two farm workers were killed. Many among the men, women, children, and babes-in-arms were injured. All who could, fled in terror. Armed local vigilantes, four companies of the National Guard, and deputized Burns Agency "detectives" arrived the next day. Throughout the state, hundreds of Wobblies were arrested, beaten, and thrown into jail. Many were held incommunicado for weeks. Ford and Suhr were tried and found guilty of murder, even though the prosecution conceded that Suhr had been in Arizona at the time of the riot. They were sentenced to life imprisonment.

The Wheatland affair was one of the most important events in the history of the California farm labor movement, in several ways. For months, the riot was discussed in newspapers and magazines throughout the state and nation, and even abroad. It was the first time most people had heard of California's industrialized agriculture, and the working and living conditions which prevailed. In response to a temporarily aroused public, the California legislature enacted a labor camp code, and created a new office of Housing and Immigration

Commissioner to enforce it. A good and conscientious man, Simon J. Lubin, was appointed commissioner by Governor Hiram Johnson. But public interest waned. Lubin, and his successors (including Carey McWilliams, from 1939 to 1943), were never given the staff they needed.

More importantly, perhaps, the Wheatland Riot gave the farm labor movement its first martyrs. The killed and injured were lost in anonymity, but the names of Blackie Ford and Herman Suhr were remembered. Wobblies stepped up their organizing around the slogan, "Free Ford and Suhr!" On hundreds of trees along the valley roads, signs appeared: "As long as Ford and Suhr are in prison, don't stick copper nails in fruit trees. It kills them." The signs were affixed with copper nails.

Even AFL members, while continuing to reject the IWW's revolutionary ideology, were momentarily stirred by the appeal to labor martyrdom, and responded to campaigns to raise funds for the defense of Ford and Suhr. Eventually, after many appeals and twelve years in prison, they were released.

The vigor of the Wobbly movement is suggested by the fact that growers mounted an unusually vigorous countermovement. Federal agents rounded up hundreds of Wobblies in 1917, on grounds of wartime disloyalty. All records and files at IWW's national headquarters in Chicago were confiscated. In 1919, largely at the behest of growers, California enacted a Criminal Syndicalism law, making it a felony to "teach, advocate, aid or abet acts of violence to effect political change"—including change in industrial ownership or control. This law was invoked, first, against the remaining Wobblies, and later against members of the Communist Party who became involved in farm labor organizing. After 1935, the law fell into disuse; local ordinances, court injunctions and restraining orders, and vigilantes were generally sufficient to put down farm labor unrest. The Criminal Syndicalism Act was not revived until the summer of 1968, in a Los Angeles civil rights case. In June, 1969, the United States Supreme Court finally ruled such state laws unconstitutional.

Even if there had been no World War I and no Criminal Syndicalism Act, the IWW could hardly have built a lasting organization of farm workers. Its appeal was largely limited to white, transient, single male workers, who have never constituted more than a small minority of the California farm labor force. What is more, the IWW's goals would ultimately have repelled most farm workers, who seek only decent wages and working conditions, and a voice in setting them, rather than any revolutionary changes in society. Whatever their shortcomings, however, the Wobblies left a significant legacy. They demonstrated that farm workers can, with appropriate techniques, be organized. Those techniques include organizing from the "grass roots" up rather than from the top down, organizing "on the job," and "solidarity" among workers in different occupations and industries.

World War I brought high profits to California growers, as wartime always does. And, as also seems true of wartime, workers' grievances were dampened by appeals to patriotism, and by flooding the farm labor market with large numbers of new workers. Some were dilettantes (housewives, students), some were semicaptives (Mexican contract workers). The effect was to prevent regular farm workers from taking advantage of the law of labor supply and demand to improve their position.

After the war, the dissatisfactions of professional agricultural workers could no longer be contained. Between 1919 and 1921, at least ten significant strikes occurred in such disparate areas as Santa Rosa, Lodi, Los Angeles, Fresno, and Brawley—some of them spontaneous, some under the leadership of the AFL, some under lingering adherents of the IWW who now called themselves "Toilers of the World."

The usual postwar recession, however, effectively ended farm workers' militancy. There was no such thing as public welfare or social insurance in the sense we know it today. Marginal workers gravitated to cities when times were good, and back to rural areas when times were bad, filling the farm labor pool to overflowing. Furthermore, the sharp decline in farm prices in 1921 enabled growers to claim, with some justice, that they could not afford to improve wages. A seven-year period of comparative farm labor "peace" ensued.

In 1928, that peace was broken from an unexpected quarter. California growers—particularly those in the Southern portions of the state—by now were taking for granted their labor supply from Mexico. Either they did not know or did not care what Spanish-speaking farm labor contractors did about such amenities as drinking water in the fields. They did not know or did not care what kinds of conditions Mexicans lived under, with their families, on the banks of irrigation ditches. They had no idea of where or how their workers spent the months when their labor was not needed. The "homing pigeon" myth was one of many which growers used to convince themselves everyone was contented. But most Mexicans had no real home to return to after the harvest. They tended to huddle together in wretched *barrios,* in unincorporated areas around such cities as Los Angeles, depending on charity or an occasional odd job to get through the off-seasons.

"The Mexican . . . possesses a great capacity for happiness," rhapsodized one grower spokesman. But their great capacity was not for happiness—it was for endurance, learned through generations of experience on the haciendas of Mexico, under the *patrón* system. If one were born on a hacienda with a kindly patrón (master), one could look forward to a tolerable life, pleased with one's good fortune. If one were born on a hacienda with a cruel, miserly patrón . . . well, that was too bad, but there was nothing to be done about it. One took refuge behind *vacilada*—a mask to cover disappointment. One shrugged; one made a wry joke as an alternative to despair. Whatever the event, good luck or bad, it was out of one's own hands: the patrón made all the decisions governing one's life.

For many years, California agriculture has capitalized on this cultural heritage. But the endurance of peons, although great, is not unlimited. Sometimes they revolted in Old Mexico. And sometimes in California.

On the eve of the picking season in May, 1928, Imperial Valley cantaloupe growers were astonished to receive several demands from their "contented" Mexican workers, who had quietly been organizing since the previous November. The organization was called La Unión de Trabajadores del Valle Imperial; later it changed its name to the Mexican Mutual Aid Society.

The demands were few and courteously worded: a modest, standardized increase in the piece rate; insurance against on-the-job accidents; free picking sacks; iced drinking water in the fields, where temperatures usually rose well above 100 degrees. Union leaders had hoped to settle the issues through arbitration; they had no strike plans. But when growers refused to dignify the requests with a reply, some members went on strike spontaneously. Wholesale arrests, jailings, and deportations soon brought an end to the immediate "trouble."

The workers' principal grievance, however, was the labor contractor system, and this issue was not so easily swept aside. The union addressed a petition to the state Division of Labor Law Enforcement and to "the American Public in General," pleading for help in ending the depredations of contractors. "The Mexican is becoming the prey of professional despoilers," the petition stated, pointing out that the contractors regularly pocketed from a fourth to a half of their crews' earnings, and sometimes absconded with the entire payroll. A state investigation corroborated the workers' complaints, and revealed numerous additional violations as well.

The state Division of Labor Law Enforcement drew up a "standard picking agreement," in which it proposed to clarify a long-standing confusion by establishing the grower, rather than the contractor, as the responsible employer. Since the Division had no authority to enforce this agreement, it came to little more than the efforts of the workers themselves. Afterward, however, Imperial Valley and other growers were never again quite so smug about Mexicans' "great capacity for happiness." For their part, the Mexican workers had learned a good deal about banding together for common ends. The Imperial Valley incident also gave the farm labor movement another memorable name: Carlos Ariza, consul of the Republic of Mexico and principal organizer of the Mexican Mutual Aid Society.

The following year, 1929, saw the beginning of the Depression. To nonagricultural workers throughout the nation, the 1930's brought joblessness, hunger, and anxiety, but also a renascence of union organizing which, coupled with new, pro-labor legislation, resulted finally in permanent organizations and economic gains. To agricultural labor, the 1930's brought unemployment, hunger, insecurity, and unprecedented organizing efforts, too. But there were to be no pro-labor laws or permanent gains for farm workers.

In September, 1929, just a month before the Wall Street crash, the Communist Party U.S.A. set up a Trade Union Unity League to organize farm laborers and other unorganized mass-production workers, essentially untouched by the AFL. The TUUL did not have to wait long for its first test in California agriculture.

In January, 1930, large numbers of Mexican vegetable workers left their jobs in the Imperial Valley. Most of them were former members of the Mexican Mutual Aid Association. This time, they were joined by workers from other ethnic groups: perhaps as many as 5,000 in all. The *Daily Worker* called it "the beginning of mass rebellion by all the scores of thousands of bitterly exploited Mexican, Filipino, Hindu, Japanese, and Chinese agricultural laborers who slave for the big open-shop fruit growers and packers . . ." The TUUL dispatched organizers to take charge of the "revolutionary situation." But the situation was not revolutionary, any more than there were still "Chinese agricultural laborers" in the fields at that time. Communist organizers won a contest with the local leadership, which confused the workers and gave growers an excuse to cry "Bolshevism," and violently to suppress the movement with the support of virtually the entire community. The strike collapsed.

It was a pattern to be repeated, in its essential outlines, for four years, although as time went by the Communist organizers gained finesse and were not so crude in taking over spontaneous local demonstrations of unrest. A front called the Agricultural Workers Industrial League was established. It became involved in four major strikes in the next two years, all of which were short-lived and unsuccessful. In July, 1931, the AWIL was changed to Cannery and Agricultural Workers Industrial Union, or CAWIU, and it was prominent in some of the largest and bloodiest strikes in the history of American agriculture.

By 1933, it seemed that every inland valley and coastal plain of California was aflame with farm worker protests. No one knows how many small, local work stoppages went unrecorded that year; 37 strikes were important enough to appear in the records of government agencies. An estimated total of 47,575 workers walked off their jobs, or were locked out, with 669,400 man-days lost. Of these 37 major strikes, 24 came under the leadership of the CAWIU, including all of the major ones. Two were led by AFL affiliates; two by organizations unaffiliated with either the AFL or CAWIU; three by unknown leadership; six began spontaneously, and remained under the control of the workers directly involved.

A strike of cotton pickers in the lower San Joaquin Valley in October, 1933, was the largest and most dramatic of them all. It was unusual, among other respects, in the amount of planning which preceded it. The growers' long-standing practice of meeting in advance of the season and setting a "prevailing wage" played into the hands of CAWIU organizers. Before a single boll was picked, they had several weeks in which to harness worker resentment of the 60 cents per hundred rate the Agricultural Labor Bureau had agreed upon. The union demanded $1.00 a hundredweight, which had been the prevailing rate as recently as 1930.

Growers also played into the union's hands in precipitously evicting all strikers from camps and ditch banks on company property. The union had farsightedly rented forty acres of open land near Corcoran, and strikers moved there in large numbers. This provided a ready-made "staging area" for roving picket lines conducted by automobile —a technique necessitated by the far-flung strike zone, and one to be used in many subsequent farm labor strikes.

The strike spread to as many as 15,000 workers across three counties. About three-fourths of the cotton pickers were Spanish-speaking, and in a subsequent report, Paul Taylor and Clark Kerr, of the University of California, described the union's appeals:

> The excitement of the parades, the fiery talks, the cheering, appealed to the Mexicans particularly, and race discrimination, poor housing, and low pay . . . were rallying cries which appealed to a class of workers with adequate personal experience to vivify the charges hurled by Communist leaders and rendered exposition of the theories of Karl Marx superfluous.

The strike was marked by growers' violence almost from the start. In an ambush of farm workers leaving a union meeting in Pixley, two were killed, several others badly wounded. Newspapers called the ambush a "riot," and seventeen strike leaders were arrested and jailed for weeks. Eleven growers were arrested but acquitted in the local court. By the end of the strike, another worker had been shot to death, 42 had been wounded, nine children had died of malnutrition, and 113 strikers had been arrested.

Public sympathy was aroused as it had not been since the Wheatland Riot of twenty years before. Urban liberals, students, clergymen, and even some small growers supported the cotton workers. Public sentiment and representatives of the NRA (National Recovery Administration) prevailed on Governor James Rolph to appoint a mediation board. Its recommendation of 75 cents a hundredweight was accepted by the strikers and, reluctantly, by the growers.

In all, 29 of 1933's major agricultural strikes ended in some gains for the workers. Almost without exception, these gains took the form of modest wage increases. In no case did a grower or group of growers formally recognize the existence of a union.

The CAWIU led or strongly influenced ten strikes in 1934, but they were small, of short duration, and in different crop areas from the activities of 1933. By the summer of 1934, CAWIU was for all practical purposes dead. Such factors as the following contributed to its demise.

(1) Growers "bought off" workers' discontent by unilaterally raising wages from an average of about 15 cents an hour to as much as 20 cents an hour.

(2) In no case did the CAWIU leave behind it a stable organization to build upon the accomplishments of 1933. Like other Communist groups, its structure was characterized by "democratic centralism," with the center reserved for Party members. The 1934 CAWIU convention recognized as much:

> Probably the outstanding shortcoming of the leadership of the 1933 struggles was that too large a part of the leadership consisted of comrades who were not native to the situation that existed, and did not know the territorial conditions of the industry, or the relation of the contending forces.

(3) The Party faithful were torn between a revolutionary ideology and day-to-day realities which often called for moderation and compromise.

(4) The undisguised Communist affiliations of CAWIU leaders gave growers an opportunity to enlist the support of other industries, the American Legion, law enforcement agencies, and many citizens who might have remained neutral in an ordinary labor-management contest, or even sympathized with the workers, but could be stampeded by the Communist scare. A few months after the great cotton strike of 1933, representatives of the state Chamber of Commerce, Farm Bureau Federation, University of California College of Agriculture, and others conceived an organization for the express purpose of putting down agricultural strikes. This organization became known

as Associated Farmers, Inc. Throughout the remainder of the 1930's, Associated Farmers fought farm unionism with methods which often verged on fascistic, arguing that the end of combating Red sedition justified any means.

(5) On July 20, 1934, all the top leaders of the CAWIU were arrested under California's Criminal Syndicalism law. They were held for nine months awaiting trial. Eight, including all the key district organizers, were convicted and sentenced to several years' imprisonment. The CAWIU was formally dissolved on March 17, 1935.

Whatever else may be said about the period of Communist leadership of the California farm labor movement, more names survive than was true of earlier periods in the movement. Key organizers included Lillian Monroe (sometimes called "the most beautiful Communist in America"), Pat Chambers, and Caroline Decker. The fact that large numbers of farm workers sometimes followed their leadership did not mean that farm workers themselves were interested in or "duped" by Communist doctrine. The most significant aspect of the "revolutionary" period of the farm labor movement is that it was not, in fact, revolutionary. Communist leaders were followed only to the extent they articulated the modest desires of workers, quite within the framework of capitalism and constitutional democracy: tolerable wages and conditions, security of person, freedom of association.

Most farm workers were unsophisticated, lacking in organizational and public-speaking skills. They were willing to follow people who had such skills and made them available without any apparent strings attached. Marxism meant nothing to farm laborers. All they wanted was an ordinary union. They did not understand what the Associated Farmers and newspapers of the state were shouting about. For a few, faith in "the American way" was tested beyond the breaking point. All things considered, however, one of the most remarkable aspects of the farm labor movement has been its continuing trust in the American promise. Workers in industrialized agriculture, sometimes called the last proletariat, have simply refused to behave as Marxist theory says a proletariat should.

A cornerstone of President Franklin D. Roosevelt's plan for economic recovery was the right of workers to organize and bargain collectively through unions of their own choosing. The National Industrial Recovery Act, passed in his "first 100 days," incorporated this right. The NIRA was ruled unconstitutional by the "nine old men" of the United States Supreme Court. The National Labor Relations (Wagner) Act was then passed, in 1935, and upheld under Article I, Section 8(3)—the "commerce clause"—of the constitution.

John L. Lewis, head of the powerful United Mine Workers, argued in the inner circles of the AFL that the NIRA and NLRA were a magna carta to organize workers who had always fallen through the interstices of the AFL's guild philosophy. A worker who tightened a bolt on an automobile assembly line was not exactly a machinist; one who tacked on the upholstery was not a furniture maker; one who installed the windows was not really a candidate for the glaziers' union. Why not organize them all into a single union of automobile workers, along with the painters, janitors, clerks, and everybody else who worked in the plant? In 1935, Lewis formed a Committee for Industrial Organization within the AFL.

The idea was too advanced, and Lewis's personality too abrasive, for most AFL leaders. In 1937, Lewis walked out, was pushed out, or both, and the CIO became the Congress of Industrial Organizations, with no ties to the AFL. It was a time of dizzying progress in union-building. Lewis required no loyalty oaths, other than loyalty to industrial unionism. Any viable organization of industrial workers could get a CIO charter, it seemed—and even some which were not so viable.

Leftists had not totally abandoned the field with the collapse of the CAWIU in 1934. Under a revised Party line, they had tried to "bore from within" some small farm workers' unions which were affiliated with the AFL. After the split between the AFL and CIO, there was no doubt which way they would go. At a convention in Denver in July, 1937, representatives from some fifty-two locals, from eleven states, formed a national committee which was shortly chartered by the CIO as the United Cannery, Agricultural, Packing, and Allied Workers of America (UCAPAWA). A New York intellectual named Donald Henderson managed to get himself named president of UCAPAWA. His critics said, "If he's not a card-carrying Communist, he's cheating the Party out of his dues. And he's never been any closer to agriculture than Central Park."

For the rest of the 1930's, the farm labor movement in California was slowed by jurisdictional wrangling between UCAPAWA and the AFL. Most of the CIO's effort was directed toward organizing auxiliary and ancillary workers, under the plausible theory that growers would be forced to come to terms if cannery and packingshed workers, longshoremen, warehousemen, and others refused to handle "hot" produce. A good many cannery workers and dried-fruit workers were organized. The AFL, however, held one very powerful card: the Teamsters. The CIO had nothing to challenge the fact that produce must move from fields to canneries, from canneries to docks, from warehouses to retail stores, on wheels. The Teamsters exercised unquestioned hegemony over these key links in the food chain. Through this leverage, the AFL obtained more contracts than the CIO in agriculture-related industries, even though the CIO was generally more successful in the preliminary organizing. Cannery workers ended up in the Teamsters union, with several key assists from the National Labor Relations Board. Dairy workers were absorbed by the Teamsters. Winery workers went into another AFL affiliate.

Field workers tended to be lost in the jurisdictional jockeying, and in the strategy which called for establishment of an organizational base "under a roof," first, before moving out into the fields. Throughout the 1930's, there continued to be local strikes, but most were spontaneous and independent of either the AFL or CIO: potato diggers in Santa Barbara County, apple pickers in Sonoma County, pea pickers in Yolo County, grape packers in Merced County, artichoke workers in the Santa Cruz area, and others. The number of work stoppages significant enough to come to the attention of government agencies declined from twenty-four in 1936 to fifteen in 1937 and thirteen in 1938.

Most of these strikes were unsuccessful even in winning temporary pay increases. To the jurisdictional problem within the house of labor was added an equally serious problem from outside: Associated Farmers, Inc., was growing in power, zeal, and experience in stamping out "agitation." The final major strike of the decade is a fair illustration of the genre. Cotton had brought the agricultural strike wave of 1933 to its climax; cotton was again the crop involved in the last great strike of the Depression period.

Madera County, in the middle of the San Joaquin Valley, was a stronghold of the Associated Farmers. The "prevailing rate" for the

1939 cotton harvest was set in advance at 80 cents a hundredweight. Pickers demanded $1.25. Growers refused to meet with workers' representatives to discuss the issue. The newly elected governor, liberal Democrat Culbert L. Olson, vainly attempted to mediate. The growers prepared for a showdown. They induced the county board of supervisors to pass the Associated Farmers' "best ordinance." One of its provisions required pickets to obtain a "parade" permit from the sheriff, which would certainly be refused. This dodge was designed to prevent car caravans, the union's stock-in-trade.

Unionists organized car caravans, anyway, and were put in jail. That did not halt the daily picketing along back roads bordering the cotton fields or the nightly union meetings in Madera's public park. Strike leaders were arrested on grounds of "criminal conspiracy," a felony, for advocating violation of the anti-picketing ordinance. The union claimed that the strike was still 90 percent effective.

Urged on by the local newspaper, which advocated lynching the strike leaders, growers set up an emergency committee to "break loose" and "give it the works." On the morning of October 26, as picket cars began to move, a two-hundred-car caravan of growers appeared. Pickets were set upon and beaten with fists and rubber hoses. That evening, when the workers attempted to meet as usual in the park, they were attacked by some three hundred growers armed with axe handles. State highway patrolmen fired tear gas into the crowd to "quiet the melee"—an intriguing reminiscence of the philosophy of crowd control and choice of phrases used at Wheatland.

The union local was broken, although with the help of Governor Olson, a compromise wage offer of $1.00 per hundredweight was eventually put into effect.

After World War II, a CIO successor to UCAPAWA, the Food, Tobacco and Agricultural Workers Union, known as FTA, attempted to return to California and pick up the pieces left over from the 1930's. FTA had considerable success in canneries, but the combination of the Teamsters and an NLRB which was biased in favor of the Teamsters, was too much to overcome. It was the final effort to organize California's food complex along industrial union lines. Soon afterward, FTA was expelled from the CIO for alleged Communist domination.

MILLS COLLEGE
LIBRARY

During all the jurisdictional tugging and hauling, some ethnic groups had continued to organize themselves. The most effective of these groups, and the most consistently ignored by both the AFL and CIO, were the Filipinos. They had long since banded themselves into crews which functioned under leaders who represented their interests, in much the same way as the old Japanese crews.

The Filipino crews became models of cooperation and efficiency. They were able to outproduce all other workers in such specialty crops as asparagus and Brussels sprouts, and gained a virtual labor monopoly in these crops. They began to talk about taking advantage of this monopoly position. Some Filipinos leaned toward the AFL, more to the CIO, but even more were attracted to the idea of an independent, nationalistic union. In March, 1938, a conference of all Filipino organizations on the Pacific Coast was called by a personal representative of President Manuel Quezon of the Philippine Islands. The result was a Filipino Agricultural Workers Association, later known as the Filipino Agricultural Labor Association (FALA).

After a year of organizing, FALA made its first demands, in the asparagus harvest of the San Joaquin–Sacramento delta. The harvest was just reaching its peak; growers were caught completely by surprise; efforts to recruit whites, Negroes, or Mexicans would have failed, and the growers knew it. A one-day work stoppage was sufficient. All 258 asparagus growers signed agreements with FALA.

During the rest of 1939, FALA achieved other successes: Brussels sprouts in San Mateo County; celery in San Joaquin County; garlic in San Benito County. In 1940, growers were better prepared, and fought back. Seeking added strength, FALA members voted to affiliate with the AFL. The drive became bogged down in legal disputes, although it had some success in stopping the commonplace practice of deducting "holdbacks" from wages, to be paid only if a worker stayed throughout the entire season.

The coup de grace was given FALA by Japan's invasion of the Philippines. Thousands of patriotic Filipinos joined the U.S. armed forces, where they were usually relegated to positions as mess "boys." Those who remained in agriculture bent themselves to helping the war through food production. But the movement had provided more leaders whose names are remembered: Chris Mensalves and Dr. Macario Bautista, among others.

The course of every social movement is affected profoundly by outside events over which it has no control. At many turns, the farm labor movement was adversely affected by wars, depressions, and other broad national and international trends. Of these, none worked more fatefully against farm labor organization than World War II. Despite the errors and floundering of the movement in the 1930's, progress had been made. Thoughtful Americans had become aware of the nature of industrial agriculture, and most were sympathetic to the workers' position. Growers could hire public relations firms, but they could not hire anyone with the writing power and passion of a Steinbeck or a McWilliams.

Late 1939 and early 1940 brought one of the most promising developments in the history of the farm labor movement to that point. Senator Robert La Follette, Jr., of Wisconsin, nominally a Republican, but actually one of the country's outstanding liberals, chaired a series of hearings on "Violations of Free Speech and Rights of Labor." The La Follette committee had an excellent staff, headed by Henry Fowler, who later became Secretary of the Treasury. The committee spent much of its time in California, taking testimony on violations of the constitutional rights of agricultural workers at Madera, Stockton, Salinas, in the Imperial Valley, and virtually everywhere else they had tried to organize. Although farm workers were excluded from the Wagner Act, they were still presumably entitled to the constitutional guarantees of speech and assembly.

There was another significant thrust in the La Follette committee's investigation. Public support for the National Industrial Recovery Act and Wagner Act had been gained, in large part, through the argument that without collective bargaining machinery, strife and violence prevailed in industry, and public peace could only be restored by provision for the orderly settlement of labor disputes. Laymen might not fully grasp the fine points of equity in bargaining strength and the distribution of purchasing power, but they understood bloodshed when they saw it; they did not like it, and they supported a law which promised to put an end to it.

In these terms, the La Follette committee built a potent case for the extension of the Wagner Act to agriculture. Friends of the farm labor movement could say, "We were excluded from the original Wagner Act on the grounds that agriculture was not an industry and didn't need industrial relations machinery. But here's proof it does need such machinery. It's going through precisely the same kind of turmoil that other industries went through before they were required to start holding representation elections."

Had history not intervened, this argument, backed by thousands of blood-stained pages of evidence, might have carried the day. The La Follette committee's recommendations, calling for orderly collective bargaining in agriculture, did not appear in the Congressional Record until October 19, 1942. By then the opportunity was gone. In wartime Washington, nobody was concerned about "labor peace" in agriculture. Indeed, growers had already taken advantage of the situation to institute the bracero program, which was tantamount to a gilt-edged insurance policy against unionism in agriculture.

This episode had an even more ironic ending. After the war, Senator La Follette might have taken up his interest in the rights of farm workers again. But, in 1946, one of the most constructive of senators was defeated by a man who was to prove one of the most destructive —Joseph McCarthy.

3. To Build a Union

With the end of World War II, rationing, price and wage controls, and other wartime emergency programs were lifted. But one wartime program lingered on. Claiming that they continued to suffer an acute "labor shortage," California growers obtained Congressional extension of the bracero system, year after year. It guaranteed a superabundant, semicaptive, alien labor force, which was the best of all possible guarantees against organization of domestic farm workers. Growers were thus unprepared when the serpent of unionization reappeared in their private Eden in the summer of 1947, in the form of the National Farm Labor Union.

The NFLU was a direct outgrowth of the Southern Tenant Farmers Union, founded by H. L. Mitchell and others in Arkansas in 1934. Initially, the STFU's major efforts were directed toward the U.S. Department of Agriculture, to prevent the new Agricultural Adjustment Act from being abused by Southern plantation owners. The Act introduced the principle of price stabilization through acreage reduction. Many planters kept their entire allotment for themselves, leaving tenants and sharecroppers with "retired acreage," on which they were now forbidden, under penalty of law, to grow their own cash crop, cotton.

From its very first meeting, the STFU constituted a living challenge to the most basic traditions of its region. It was racially integrated; it was committed to nonviolence; and it subscribed to an indigenous variety of democratic socialism. Ignoring the sectarian warfare of the time between Stalinism and Trotskyism, STFU raised an issue which had real meaning to its members: land for the landless.

STFU attracted the support of the American Civil Liberties Union and the League for Industrial Democracy, gained the ear of Eleanor Roosevelt, led directly to the founding of the National Sharecroppers Fund, and awakened much of the nation to the fact that, in the post-Reconstruction period, the South had devised institutions closely resembling outright serfdom: sharecropping and tenant farming.

As more and more "croppers" were evicted and became day laborers, STFU turned to the problems of wage workers. For a short time, STFU tried to function within the United Cannery, Agricultural, Packing, and Allied Workers of America (UCAPAWA), but as Mitchell put it, "Those fellows were a lot more interested in whitewashing the Stalin purges and fighting the Spanish Civil War than in organizing farm workers."

STFU turned from the CIO to the AFL. William Green, long-time AFL president, took a personal interest in the struggling, idealistic STFU. In 1945, it was chartered as the National Farm Labor Union, largely through Green's good offices. The NFLU issued him its Membership Book No. 1, and he remained an honorary member until his death.

In 1947, NFLU leaders raised enough money to expand beyond their base in the Mississippi Delta. They turned westward. They decided to start with a bellwether of California agribusiness, the Di Giorgio Fruit Company. Early in July, organizing began in the vicinity of Arvin, southeast of Bakersfield in Kern County, where Joseph Di Giorgio, founder of the dynasty, had his home ranch. The choice was not haphazard. Di Giorgio's ranch contained 10,621 acres. In the fields and orchards, in packing sheds (one was a quarter of a mile long), and in one of the largest wineries in the world, about eight hundred workers were employed the year round, and another sixteen hundred during the autumn harvest peak. Di Giorgio had a reputation as a particularly energetic and effective foe of farm labor unionism. NFLU strategists calculated that if the bellwether could be organized, the rest of the industry would follow.

Conditions for Di Giorgio's field workers were no worse than those in the industry generally; in certain material respects they were probably better. But the workers objected to paternalism, just as plantation workers in Hawaii were rejecting paternalism and joining the International Longshoremen's and Warehousemen's Union at about this same time. Di Giorgio employees objected to the company towns, the company stores, and the many decisions affecting their lives made unilaterally by the company. Organizing efforts by NFLU's Local 218 progressed rapidly. By September, 1947, members agreed on four basic demands: a wage increase of ten cents an hour, grievance procedures, the principle of seniority, and a union contract. Every attempt to bring union and company representatives together—by the union itself, by the Kern County Central Labor Council, by federal and state conciliators—came to nothing. The company refused to admit the existence of the union.

On September 30, the membership voted to strike. Picket lines appeared the next morning. The union's effort became known as the "world's longest picket line," for the public roads surrounding the huge ranch covered nearly twenty miles. The picket line also proved to be among the world's longest in point of time; it was maintained daily, except Sundays, for over two and a half years.

Union-breaking actions by the company and its allies were somewhat different from those of the 1930's. The "red scare" was still used, and sporadic violence was directed against strikers—one leader was shot by night riders and badly wounded—but agribusiness had become more conscious of its "image," and the importance of good public relations. No paramilitary grower battalions were organized; they were not needed. The company turned increasingly to more sophisticated techniques.

Just one week before the NFLU began organizing in Arvin, Congress had passed the Taft-Hartley Act over President Truman's veto. The new law weakened some of the Wagner Act's liberal provisions, jettisoned some entirely, and added some major restrictions on union activity. In an astonishing interpretation, a National Labor Relations Board examiner ruled that farm laborers could be disciplined under the Act, and proscribed from certain picketing and boycott activities, even though they were excluded from all the benefits of the Act. This interpretation was later overturned at a higher level, but it hurt the union gravely during much of the strike.

Another powerful weapon available to Di Giorgio, which had not been available in the 1930's, was the government's Mexican labor program. When the strike began, 130 braceros were employed on the Arvin ranch. They stopped work in sympathy with the local laborers, but after visits from a Mexican consul, the Kern County sheriff, and a field representative from the U.S. Department of Agriculture, they went back to work. The persuasion was very simple: "Work or be deported." Since strikebreaking was explicitly forbidden by the braceros' master contract, the union protested to friendly Congressmen, and the braceros were transferred to other growers—but not until November 10. It was the first recorded use of a technique employed repeatedly by bracero users in years to come: during a strike, keep braceros on the job, exploiting bureaucratic due process to the utmost; by the time it is ruled that the braceros are being used improperly, the harvest will be over and the whole question will be moot.

The six weeks' delay enabled Di Giorgio to keep up with harvesting and irrigating during a critical period, and gave the company time to recruit strikebreakers from as far away as Texas. The replacements were not informed that a strike was in progress. This practice was in violation of federal law, but has always been practiced with impunity by California growers. In November, the state Farm Placement Service in Bakersfield began using its tax-supported facilities to refer workers to the struck ranch, a violation of still another law. Further, at critical periods throughout the strike, Di Giorgio used wetbacks. To the extent that the Border Patrol enforced the immigration laws at all—the union claimed it was very indifferently—it was wetbacks themselves who paid the penalty, not Di Giorgio. To this day there are no penalties against employing illegal entrants, unless it can be proved the employer knows they are illegal entrants—which is almost impossible to prove.

The Di Giorgio company made judicious use of public relations methods. Company spokesmen released a stream of bland assurances to the mass media: there are no problems between the Di Giorgio company and its employees; there is no strike; there is no union; it is a figment of the imagination of outside agitators. In December, 1947, the company issued a highly professional pamphlet, "A Community Aroused," which seemed to support its claims. Only someone familiar at first hand with Di Giorgio's company town would have known that the photographs of "worker housing" were actually pictures of the trim, landscaped bungalows of supervisory personnel.

Finally, the company utilized the device of official "investigations" by legislators sympathetic to its position. The California Senate Committee on Un-American Activities came to investigate Joseph Di Giorgio's claim that "this agitation is Communist-inspired by subversive elements." The charge was too incredible for even this credulous committee: H. L. Mitchell and his co-workers had for over ten years been fighting Communist attempts to infiltrate their union.

Toward the end of the strike, the U.S. House of Representatives Committee on Education and Labor appointed a three-man subcommittee to look into the Di Giorgio affair and the question of whether collective bargaining laws should be extended to agribusiness. On this subcommittee was a sophomore congressman from California named Richard Nixon. In March, 1950, Nixon signed a document asserting that farm workers had been properly excluded from labor laws, and "it would be harmful to the public interest and to all responsible labor unions to legislate otherwise." In the farm labor movement, this became known as the "Nixon Doctrine."

For its part, the NFLU was working out new techniques, too. The union developed a network of support from organized labor, the clergy, students and teachers, and liberals throughout the country. Ministers from San Francisco and Los Angeles visited the picket lines and returned to the cities to urge their congregations to help. Students from the University of California at Berkeley made pilgrimages to Arvin. The "old curmudgeon," former Secretary of the Interior Harold L. Ickes, issued a release stating that Di Giorgio's workers lived in a condition of "serfdom." Early in February, 1948, a National Citizens Committee to support the strike was formed by Norman Thomas, John Dos Passos, Robert Hutchins, and others.

Car caravans organized by members of Los Angeles and San Francisco central labor councils regularly brought food, clothing, and money to the union's headquarters in Arvin. Various central labor bodies, local unions, internationals, and state federations of labor sent monthly contributions. Altogether, the labor movement contributed an estimated $80,000 to NFLU's Local 218, and the equivalent of even more in food, clothing, and other contributions. The strike became a movement which transcended geographic and occupational lines, which embraced people from many walks of life who were bound together by a common sense of justice, and by the drama which is always inherent when a seemingly hopeless underdog challenges an overdog.

From the drama in Arvin, names emerged. The president of the local, shot and seriously wounded by night riders, was James Price. The head organizer, dispatched from NFLU Eastern headquarters, was Hank Hasiwar. Toward the end of the strike, a new name appeared: Dr. Ernesto Galarza, newly appointed Director of Research and Education for the union. The California farm labor movement would not again sink into anonymity.

The union had organized most of the company's field workers and three-fourths of its shed workers, but could not cope with the unrestricted importation of strikebreakers, spirited into the ranch at night. If union organizers tried to reach strikebreakers in the only way they could—in company fields or housing—they were subject to arrest for trespassing.

And the union did not have the resources to match the company's platoons of lawyers. Several Hollywood guilds donated their services to a pro-union film entitled "Poverty in the Valley of Plenty." The Di Giorgio Fruit Company filed a multimillion-dollar libel suit. Although the film was actually quite sober and restrained, and seemed secured by the First Amendment, the company won its case. No monetary damages were imposed, but the union was required to withdraw the picture from circulation, and to locate and destroy all prints. The company obtained injunctions severely limiting the union's picketing, boycotting, and assistance from other unions. The strike was finally called off in May, 1950.

NFLU did not confine its attention to the Di Giorgio Fruit Company. In September, 1949, after a two weeks' strike of several thousand cotton pickers in Tulare, Kern, Fresno, and Kings counties, the union won its demand that a pay cut from the previous year's rate of $3.00 per hundred pounds be rescinded. Among the strike leaders were William Becker and Bill Swearingen. One of the rank and file on the mobile picket line was a young man who had just turned twenty-one years old, was taking part in his first strike, and could not possibly have dreamed that sixteen years later he would be leading a far more ambitious effort. His name was Cesar Chavez.

The NFLU organized California farm workers in a number of other crop areas. Its last major victory was probably a 1952 strike on the 5,000-acre ranch of the Schenley Corporation near Delano. The union won a wage increase, and even more significantly, the establishment of grievance machinery and the re-employment of workers who had been locked out because of union activity. Fourteen years later, the Schenley ranch would again be the scene of a milestone in the farm labor movement.

With the end of the Di Giorgio strike, outside support for the NFLU dropped off to almost nothing. The state federation of labor, which had been contributing $500 a month, cut off its contribution and increased the salary of its chief executive officer by the same amount. But it was not the loss of financial support which hurt the NFLU most. With the Korean War as an excuse, growers began flooding the state with unprecedented numbers of braceros, as state and federal agencies cooperated complaisantly.

In 1955, the NFLU changed its name to National Agricultural Workers Union. During the STFU-NFLU-NAWU's closing years, Ernesto Galarza was its sole representative in California. His primary energies were devoted not to organizing but to fighting the bracero system, and trying to retain the jurisdiction of his union against the claims of other labor organizations.

When the Food, Tobacco, and Agricultural Workers Union was expelled from the CIO in 1951, its jurisdiction was given to the United Packinghouse Workers of America. At about the same time, the bracero program began to boom and grower-shippers began to move operations formerly performed in packing sheds into the fields: the trimming and packing of lettuce, celery, carrots, and the like. Shed workers had been organized with some success into Local 78, but when UPWA representatives attempted to follow the shed operations into the fields, they learned that the front lines of the farm labor battle were no longer in Salinas or the Imperial Valley but in Sacramento and Washington, D.C., where state and federal officials were deciding that braceros could be used not only in jobs formerly held by American field workers, but in jobs formerly held by American packinghouse workers.

UPWA organizers collected literally hundreds of affidavits from American citizens attesting that they had been displaced from their jobs by braceros. The U.S. Department of Labor and California Farm Placement Service denied it. The law said there was not supposed to be any displacement—therefore, obviously, no displacement could be taking place. The union had no avenue of appeal above Department of Labor officials who had themselves helped create the bracero program.

Forced to devise new techniques to deal with a labor-busting system unique in American labor history, Clive Knowles and other UPWA leaders experimented with educational picketing, demonstrations, and, on at least one occasion, a sit-in. Many "quickie" strikes were called for the announced objective of removing braceros from local workers' jobs, but, in all likelihood, more for the purpose of attracting attention to the existence of the bizarre system. For a time, these strikes helped educate the public, and served warning on growers and government agencies that they could not operate totally without scrutiny. But soon the mass media no longer found such demonstrations novel and newsworthy.

By 1959, the future looked unrelievedly bleak for both UPWA and NAWU. Then, hope flickered again. An Agricultural Workers Organizing Committee (AWOC) which, it was proudly claimed, would "do the job at last," was formed by the AFL-CIO.

According to official accounts, George Meany and other AFL-CIO leaders, out of their deep concern to right an old wrong, had created this bold program to organize the unorganized. Some Eastern liberals felt that they had pressured Meany into it by creating a National Advisory Committee on Farm Labor, which held public hearings in Washington, D.C., in February, 1959. But Franz Daniel, Assistant Director of Organization for the AFL-CIO, later told an AWOC staff meeting, "Don't kid yourself. Meany just got tired of going to international conventions and being needled by labor people from smaller, poorer foreign countries, who could point out that at least they had organized farm workers, while the American labor movement hadn't. He set up AWOC to get them off his back."

Whatever its motivations, the AWOC plan sounded impressive. More money than ever before was to be made available, and it was to be put on a predictable footing through per capita contributions by every AFL-CIO affiliate. The drive would begin in California, would move from there into Oregon and Washington, then spread across the Southwest and into the Southeast. The goal was a single union for all the agricultural workers in the country. Since there were well over two million of them at the time, this would make it substantially the largest bona fide union in the world—larger than the Teamsters who then held that distinction, and still do.

Jack Livingston, AFL-CIO Director of Organization, came to California, consulted with Ernesto Galarza, organizer-priests Thomas McCullough and Donald McDonnell, and others, and decided that AWOC headquarters would be in Stockton. To begin with, organizational efforts would be conducted within an area shaped roughly like half a pie, running about a hundred miles north, south, and west of Stockton.

Urban friends of the farm labor movement thought this was all the movement had needed over the years: experienced, responsible, hard-headed, professional organizers, backed by large amounts of money. The fate of AWOC, however, was actually sealed before the organizing drive began. The choice of director was left up to Livingston. To avoid hard feelings, he decided not to choose a representative of either NAWU or UPWA, but a "new face." This eliminated everybody who had had any significant experience with agricultural workers. And when he looked for a leader among other arms of the labor movement, he found no one who was willing to leave the security of an established union.

At length, Livingston turned to a "new face" who was sixty-two years old: Norman Smith. Smith had had no connection with organized labor for eighteen years, during most of which he was a supervisor with the Kaiser Steel Company in Fontana, California. He had had no connection with agriculture since leaving his father's family farm in Missouri almost half a century before. But he had been involved in organizing automobile workers in the 1930's. He had plucked Jack Livingston off a General Motors assembly line and given him his start in the labor movement. Livingston thought he was returning the favor, twenty-five years later, by giving Smith the chance to obtain the recognition which had eluded him in the factional infighting between Homer Martin, R. J. Thomas, the Reuther brothers, and other early leaders of the United Automobile Workers.

In some ways, Smith was almost a stereotype of a labor organizer from an earlier era. He carried nearly three hundred pounds on his five feet eight inches and rolled like a bear as he walked. He was an indefatigable talker; given a microphone, he could hold forth for hours. In any difference of opinion, he could roar with the best of them. In other respects, however, he was no stereotype. He did not smoke, drink, or gamble. He had no interest in sports, movies, television, card-playing, hunting, fishing, or any of the other common masculine forms of recreation. He never married. His life was centered, single-mindedly, around the ideals and dynamics of the labor movement as he had known it in the 1930's. His idea of recreation was to swap yarns about those years with other old-timers.

In explaining his choice of Smith, Livingston boasted, "He could go into a graveyard and come out with an organization." Old labor jokes do not build new unions, however. It was desperately unfair to Smith to thrust him into a situation for which he was nearly totally unequipped. There was no relationship between family farming in Missouri before World War I and California agriculture in mid-century, and none between organizing auto workers at River Rouge and farm workers along the River San Joaquin.

The automobile industry had been covered by the Wagner Act and would probably not have been organized without it; the agricultural industry was excluded. In organizing auto workers, sheer oratory had been a favored technique. At even the vastest of the assembly plants, there were limited points of entry and exit. If an organizer waited by the gate with a sound truck, or with only his unamplified voice, every time a shift changed he could get his message to hundreds, perhaps even thousands of workers. Once this initial contact had been made, organizers could hire a hall for mass meetings, and ring the welkins in an even more favorable setting. This was essentially the only organizing technique Smith had ever known or could conceive. Sometimes, in candid moments, he talked nostalgically of the way UAW orators used to spellbind an audience and then be carried triumphantly around the hall on the shoulders of adherents. Consciously or otherwise, that was what he was trying to do in agriculture: sweep all before him with the power of the spoken word.

Through an area covering nearly 10,000 square miles, Smith drove himself relentlessly, searching for the agricultural equivalent of the River Rouge gate, and the audiences upon which orators had played in the glorious formative years of the UAW. He never found these equivalents, because there are none. Even in the most highly industrialized farms of California there is no one funnel through which workers enter or leave. Workers slip into the fields in their own cars or in contractors' buses; many, housed on the ranch, neither enter nor leave the premises at all. Shifts, in the usual industrial sense, are unknown. When payment is by piece rate—as it usually is—rather than by the hour, people may arrive and leave at almost any time. And always, geographic distances are enormous. The entire River Rouge plant could be tucked into one corner of any major corporation farm, or even a medium-sized one.

But Norman Smith prowled the highways and byways of the San Joaquin Valley, wearing himself and AWOC's automobiles out, looking for a factory gate. The closest parallel he ever found was a shape-up operated on Stockton's skid row by labor contractors and the state Farm Placement Service.

The chaos of the farm labor market has long served as a hiding place for men who are running away from something: men with prison records who cannot find other employment; men whose marriages have failed and who do not care to spend their lives paying alimony and child support; men who have drinking or other psychobiological problems. Almost anyone can get a job in a farm labor shape-up with no questions asked. There is no fingerprinting; no forms to fill out. A man will be viewed as a work animal, and treated rather less well, but he will get one thing out of the bargain: his privacy will be safe.

At the peak of the Stockton season, as many as fifteen hundred workers might get a day's work through this primitive system; in the off season, only a handful. Even at the peak, less than 5 percent of the farm workers in the area got their jobs through the shape-up, and they tended to be the least productive fraction. Growers did not depend on skid-row labor; most did not like it, want it, or use it at all. For others, being represented by a contractor's bus at the shape-up was a mere pretext they had to go through to obtain braceros. It proved to the government's satisfaction that they had made "reasonable efforts" to attract American workers.

Norman Smith became obsessed by the shape-ups in Stockton and other valley towns. In his mind, they became the "key that will unlock the whole industry." He dwelled lovingly on the similarities between farm labor shape-ups and those in the automobile industry before the CIO brought order out of planned disorder. He never perceived the crucial respects in which the analogy broke down. Nearly every morning for five years, he could be found on Stockton's skid row, beginning about 4:00 A.M., arguing, browbeating, cajoling, buying coffee, loaning money which neither he nor the borrower expected would be returned. No one will ever know how many of AWOC's two-dollar memberships were paid for by Smith himself.

What is more, Smith directed most of his organizers to do as he was doing: concentrate on "the street," as he called it. Their activities were not really organizing, in any meaningful sense of the term. A transient cannot be "organized" when he has no commitment to his occupation beyond the day immediately at hand, and, far from wanting to be involved with his fellow workers, and sacrifice for them, is trying to escape from human involvement of all kinds.

The rest of the AWOC organizers' time had almost as little to do with true organizing. It was devoted to ferreting out abuses, scandals, and law violations in the bracero program, of which there was never any dearth.

AWOC did, however, benefit from two groups which had organized themselves. One consisted of Filipinos, most of whom had formerly belonged to the Filipino Agricultural Labor Association. Although getting well along into middle age, many were still employed in asparagus, table grapes, and other specialty crops. The other group was composed of fruit tramps, many of whom had become disillusioned by the failure of previous organizing drives, but some of whom were willing to take yet another chance.

The first significant AWOC strike was in San Joaquin County cherries in May, 1960. The AWOC leadership had almost nothing to do with it. Fruit tramps, who made up the bulk of the cherry harvest labor force, noted that they were getting the same amount they had been getting for several years (less than 5 cents a pound), knew that there was a farm labor union in the vicinity, and asked, "What is a union for if not to strike for higher wages?"

AWOC was swept along, although there had been no advance preparation whatever. Many smaller growers and contractors acceded to a wage increase. But no union contracts were signed. AWOC did not seriously ask for them, and would have been at a loss if a grower had said he wanted to put his labor relations on a contractual basis.

One major producer held out: Fred Podesta, known as the "world's largest cherry grower." The fruit tramps stood firm, and Podesta was not able to recruit enough strikebreakers to harvest his entire crop. He lost nearly $100,000 worth of cherries, and sued AWOC for triple damages.

This was only the beginning of AWOC's legal woes. At about the same time, the Di Giorgio Fruit Company sued AWOC and its officers for $2 million, because the disputed motion picture "Poverty in the Valley of Plenty" had been shown at several union meetings. An AWOC staff member had somehow located a copy of the film, was unaware that all prints were supposed to have been destroyed ten years earlier, and had no way of knowing that Di Giorgio still felt so litigious. Di Giorgio was awarded damages of $150,000 by a Stockton judge who was himself from an agricultural family.

There were over a hundred "strikes" during the balance of 1960, almost all of them in ladder crops, brief, involving only a few workers. AWOC can hardly be given either credit or blame for most of them. Typically, a call came to AWOC headquarters from a fruit tramp in Orland or Winters or Modesto or Lakeport, saying that he had walked out of an orchard and wanted a representative. The demand was usually $1.25 an hour, or a comparable increase (about 15 percent) in the piece rate. In many cases, wages were raised, growers evidently feeling this was cheap insurance against unionization. In no case did AWOC demand union recognition.

With the end of the 1960 season, the departure of the ladder workers to their wintering places in Tulare County, and the virtual closing of the skid row shape-up, most AWOC staff members hoped that Smith would turn his attention to the Stockton "home guard"—the mainly Spanish-speaking workers who lived in "shoestring communities" on the urban fringe and made a living as best they could from seasonal farm work and occasional jobs in canneries. But Smith declared, "There's nothing to do around here at this time of year." In December, 1960, he led AWOC into an adventure with UPWA in the Imperial Valley, 550 miles to the south, where the winter lettuce harvest was beginning.

Although practically no organizational base existed in the Imperial Valley, AWOC and UPWA representatives located enough workers to set up picket lines. The union strategy rested almost exclusively on the hope that government agencies would honor the provisions of Public Law 78 prohibiting the use of braceros as strikebreakers. This hope was not entirely unfounded. Some government officials, apparently believing that AWOC truly had the power of Big Labor behind it, had begun to make occasional decisions favorable to domestic farm workers. A new, liberal Democratic administration was about to take national office, and the Secretary of Labor was to be Arthur Goldberg, former general counsel for the CIO and for the Industrial Union Department of the AFL-CIO.

The AWOC-UPWA strategy, however, fatally overestimated the influence of labor with the new administration, and underestimated the influence of Imperial Valley growers. At no time during the strike did the government ask growers to remove more than a few braceros, and even this the growers refused to do. Their punishment for such defiance was a fair revelation of the bracero program's enforcement machinery. When the lettuce season was over, the growers in question were denied the use of braceros for six months: a period during which they had no need for braceros.

The adventure moved toward a disastrous end. Someone in the Mexican Embassy in Washington, D.C., hinted that his government, otherwise unable to intervene, could take action if it had reason to believe that the health and safety of its nationals were in jeopardy. In one of the shabbiest hours in the history of the farm labor movement, union representatives, to make it appear braceros were in mortal danger, cached some dynamite, making sure authorities would find it. Other "organizers" ran through bracero camp barracks, punching startled Mexicans and belaboring them with broom handles.

The Mexican government promptly withdrew its citizens from the camps involved, for their own protection, but it was far too little and too late to affect lettuce production. The episode served only to give Imperial Valley growers and peace officers the excuse they had been seeking. AWOC and UPWA representatives were arrested and charged not only with battery, disturbing the peace, and trespassing but with conspiracy, a more serious offense. To obtain the release of key staff members, AWOC dipped deeply into its resources; others remained in the El Centro jail for months. A long series of investigations, hearings, and trials ultimately cost AWOC tens of thousands of dollars in attorneys' fees.

Business-minded George Meany might have been willing to accept these heavy expenses if anything had been gained from the Imperial Valley venture. But there were no contracts, no dues-paying members, no permanent reduction in the use of braceros. And although growers had been far from nonviolent, it was the union's violence which was remembered. AWOC, brawling in the sands of the Imperial Valley, seemed to many observers a black sheep, giving the entire AFL-CIO family a bad name. To mix the zoological metaphor, the straw which broke Meany's camel back, however, was the revival of an old jurisdictional dispute.

The question of which union, NAWU or UPWA, would have jurisdiction over workers organized by AWOC was seemingly settled in a memorandum of understanding signed on May 21, 1959, by H. L. Mitchell and Ralph Helstein, presidents of the respective unions. Workers in jobs formerly performed in packing sheds but now moved out-of-doors would go to UPWA; all others would go to NAWU.

Since few, if any, jobs in the Stockton area were of the type which "technological progress" and the bracero program had transferred from sheds to fields, it was generally taken for granted that persons joining AWOC during the opening phases of the drive were, in effect, joining NAWU. AWOC membership books bore the NAWU name, its oath, and its symbol of a cotton boll, a hoe, and a hand plow. The first piece of organizing literature issued by AWOC stated flatly that it had "been formed to organize farm laborers into the NAWU."

Hard-pressed to keep up its per capita payments to the national AFL-CIO, and meet its other financial obligations, NAWU wanted something more immediate and more tangible. In July, 1959, H. L. Mitchell wrote to Norman Smith, asking about the "procedure for enrolling new members" in NAWU: a polite way of asking, "What's being done with the dues?" A second letter, in October, was couched in more urgent terms, and inquired whether NAWU was being eased out in favor of UPWA.

Smith did not reply, probably because he resented Mitchell's insinuations. In the absence of any instructions from the national AFL-CIO, he was impounding all dues in a trust fund. In December, growing increasingly desperate, Mitchell addressed his inquiries directly to national Secretary-Treasurer William Schnitzler, second in command only to George Meany. There was still no reply.

The silence was broken the following month. AFL-CIO leaders, judging NAWU to be little more than a sentimental holdover from an earlier generation, had decided to consign it to oblivion. To avoid "damaging" the individuals involved, and able to think only in financial terms, the AFL-CIO leadership offered Mitchell a position as Washington lobbyist for the National Sharecroppers Fund, and Galarza a place in Jack Livingston's Department of Organization. This clumsy stratagem only roused Galarza and Mitchell to greater fury and a determination to go down with all flags flying.

Galarza immediately resigned from AWOC. In February, 1960, largely at his suggestion, the NAWU executive board offered to surrender its jurisdiction in agriculture if (1) the AFL-CIO would pledge to continue its campaign to organize farm workers until a strong union was consolidated throughout the country; (2) the identity of the farm workers' organization would be preserved within the structure of any broader union which might emerge; and (3) farm workers would be represented on the policy-making board of any such union.

These may have seemed reasonable requests, but not to George Meany. In an icy reply, he said he would make no such guarantees. NAWU concluded that this left it free to work out its own merger with a larger, stronger international union. There was little question which way NAWU would turn. Mitchell had long enjoyed fraternal relations with the Amalgamated Meatcutters and Butcher Workmen of North America. The Meatcutters had a contract of many years' standing with Seabrook Farms of New Jersey, major supplier to the Campbell Soup Company. During World War II, Mitchell's union had a mutual-aid agreement with the Meatcutters' Seabrook Farms local, under which workers from the South were given the opportunity to move to New Jersey.

In April, 1960, Galarza was placed on the Meatcutters' payroll in California, while Mitchell worked out further details of a full merger. Although the Meatcutters were an old, respectable AFL craft union—the labor tradition from which George Meany himself came—Meany was not pleased at the prospect of a two-pronged organizing drive, particularly when one prong would be led by Galarza and Mitchell, of whom he was growing less and less fond. At the AFL-CIO executive council meeting in May, 1960, Meany moved to spike Galarza's and Mitchell's guns. He directed that AWOC be reorganized as the equivalent of a national union with authority to charter its own local unions. This move had no precedent in the history of either the AFL or CIO. By definition, an organizing committee had always been understood as a temporary phenomenon which would in due course give way to a national or international union. Such was Meany's control over the council, however, that the plan was approved without recorded dissent.

The situation was now as scrambled as an omelet. Since NAWU's merger with the Meatcutters had not yet been formally consummated, NAWU still held a valid AFL-CIO charter in the same jurisdiction in which the AFL-CIO had now issued another charter. Galarza wrote at once to Schnitzler, charging the executive council with violation of the AFL-CIO constitution. The letter was not answered; the AFL-CIO went ahead with its plans.

Rules of the "new AWOC" stipulated the conditions under which local unions could be chartered, but this made no difference in the way AWOC continued to operate. No locals were ever established, nor was there any effort by Norman Smith to do so.

Merger of NAWU with the Meatcutters was completed in September, 1960. An agricultural workers' division was created within the international. Its principal representative, Mitchell, began working among "agricultural and allied industry employees," principally in Louisiana. Galarza resigned from the Meatcutters' payroll that same fall, to devote himself to writing, but his feud with AWOC and UPWA was not forgotten. When the opportunity came, he did not permit others to forget, either.

The joint foray into the Imperial Valley by AWOC and UPWA in the winter of 1960–61 seemed to Galarza to prove what he had long claimed: that Smith was "very partial toward UPWA in the . . . California agricultural organizational plan." He alerted Max Osslo, Meatcutters' vice president in California; Osslo complained to Pat Gorman, Meatcutters' president; Gorman complained to George Meany that AWOC-UPWA had invaded his union's rightful jurisdiction. The prospect that there would be no end to the squabbling, coupled with the financial disasters of the lettuce strike, convinced Meany that the entire experiment in California was a failure. In June, 1961, he announced termination of all further AFL-CIO support for AWOC.

From start to finish, the jurisdictional imbroglio was part tragedy, part farce: sad because it was unnecessary; absurd because the jurisdiction existed only on paper. The issue would never have arisen if Smith had had any sort of organizing plan under which workers who took out AWOC (NAWU) membership were molded together into enduring structures. But any such plan would have had to focus on the more stable elements within the farm labor force, rather than the most unstable.

In the last analysis, responsibility rests less with Smith than with the national AFL-CIO leadership, which at no time provided him with any useful guidance. Meany himself never troubled to ascertain whether his Department of Organization had a coherent conception of how to organize farm workers. At no time did he visit Stockton to find at firsthand whether Jack Livingston's glowing progress reports were based on substance or whether they were merely wishful thinking.

None of the disputants in the sorry jurisdictional dispute had any clear grasp of the anatomy of the farm labor force in California, its backbone, its peripheries, and how it might be organized in meaningful terms. None ever raised the appropriate questions: Who actually does farm work? when? where? how long? or any of the other practical questions through which a purely theoretical jurisdictional claim might have become translated into a viable reality.

Urban friends of the farm labor movement, unaware of the flimsiness of AWOC's structure and strategy, considered Meany's withdrawal of support a betrayal, and protested vehemently. In some ways, however, the best thing that ever happened to the organization was freedom from economic dependence on the AFL-CIO.

With professionals no longer giving orders, it became possible to do many things which they had not permitted—to use volunteer organizers, for instance, who had always been anathematized by the professionals as "unreliable" and "uncontrollable." Some of the volunteers were farm workers who organized in their spare time; others were students, or were drawn from the civil rights movement. Norman Smith stayed on, and kept several AWOC offices open by using the trust fund of dues he had been impounding for over two years. His advice was taken into account, but it was not binding on the volunteers. Since they had not been hired, they could not be fired.

Smith continued to spend most of his time on skid row. The volunteers scattered into the shoestring communities where the family workers lived. They began by identifying the problems which immediately concerned the members of the home guard, and then helped them group together to work toward solutions. Some farm workers were concerned with a "redevelopment" program which threatened to wipe out their homes. Some wanted to learn how they might secure workmen's compensation or other benefits to which they were supposedly entitled. Others were concerned with a child-care center, learning English, or converting a weed-covered lot into a playground. Organization around immediate problems such as these, it was hoped, would provide training for the incalculably more difficult problem of confronting growers with economic demands. As one volunteer put it, "We have to learn to walk before we can run the marathon."

Working with the home guard, it was possible for the volunteer organizers to take a step which AWOC professionals could not and had not, working with transients: they helped create autonomous local unions. At least half a dozen such groups began meeting regularly, electing their own officials, and making their own decisions. When so moved, for instance, they communicated directly with Secretary of Labor Goldberg, which would have been unthinkable under the AWOC of the professionals. These decentralized groups were called "area councils."

Volunteer organizers issued a biweekly newsletter, with reports from each of the area councils as well as items of more general interest. There was even a strike during AWOC's "volunteer period." Several hundred Filipino workers in the Santa Cruz County Brussels sprouts harvest called for assistance, and it was given. The strike, however, was broken by the use of braceros and other out-of-area strikebreakers.

In October, 1961, several young AWOC volunteers conducted a test of the constitutional rights of agricultural workers. They attempted to pass handbills over the fence to the braceros in a camp between Stockton and Tracy. They were beaten by the proprietors, and arrested by San Joaquin County deputy sheriffs for "disturbing the peace" and "trespassing." The American Civil Liberties Union entered the case to point out that the United States Supreme Court had repeatedly affirmed the right of union organizers, religious advocates, and other interested persons to communicate with workers in company towns, lumber camps, and the like.

The trial court in the farming community of Manteca felt that agriculture was somehow a special case and found the AWOC volunteers guilty. A state appellate court upheld the conviction. The ACLU then appealed directly to the United States Supreme Court, but that body, for reasons known only to itself, ignored its own precedents and refused to review the case. To this day, the judgment of the Manteca municipal court stands as law in California: Agricultural workers housed in private labor camps are property, without the right freely to receive communications or visitors from the outside world.

Perhaps the high point of the volunteer period was an Agricultural Workers Organizing Conference, held in December, 1961, at Strathmore, Tulare County. Officers of all area councils and members from throughout the state had an opportunity to meet one another and discuss common problems, while guest speakers described the ways these same types of problems had been dealt with in earlier phases of the farm labor movement. Keynote speaker was Norman Thomas, who recounted his experiences of nearly thirty years in the movement. Over two hundred persons attended this conference—the first gathering of its kind since the mid-1930's—and many hoped it would become an annual event. Instead, the Strathmore conference inadvertently set in motion a train of circumstances which precluded any future conferences.

The biennial AFL-CIO national convention was to open within a few days—not in a bare, badly heated, converted store in a tiny citrus town but in the flamingo-tinted super-hotels of Miami Beach. Just before the Strathmore conference adjourned, someone suggested that a hat be passed and a delegation of farm workers dispatched to Miami Beach to ask for the restoration of financial support to AWOC. The proposal was adopted, $317 was collected, four representatives were elected, and they set out at once by automobile. The volunteers who had organized the conference may have had misgivings about AFL-CIO support, but they were convinced that farm workers had a right to make their own decisions—even ill-advised ones.

The four farm workers, with just $317 for all their food, lodging, and other expenses on a transcontinental round trip, evidently touched the sensibilities—or perhaps the guilt—of many AFL-CIO delegates.

A resolution was passed in Miami Beach, asking the executive council to revive support for AWOC at the earliest possible date. In January, 1962, financial support was restored.

The professionals returned, this time headed by C. Al Green, a florid-faced, cigar-smoking veteran of the building trades; Norman Smith became second-in-command. The volunteer organizers were told to go home. The area councils were abolished in favor of a centralization which was even more rigid than before. Ties with civil rights organizations, student groups, and other community organizations were cut.

For the remainder of 1962, the AWOC apparatus was turned over largely to getting out the vote for Edmund G. (Pat) Brown, who was running for a second term as governor of California. Since the AWOC professionals knew little about reaching the only farm workers who were eligible to vote—the home guard—it is doubtful that this emphasis had much, if anything, to do with Brown's decisive victory over Richard Nixon in November. Brown himself evidently doubted it; soon after his re-inaugural, he flew to Washington to urge extension of the bracero program.

In 1963, AWOC reached the reductio ad absurdum of its fascination with skid row workers. Since these workers were unable to get to their jobs except through a farm labor contractor, why bother to talk with workers at all? Why not simply "lean on" the contractors?—a technique which Green had seen used with telling effect in the building trades. This became virtually the extent of AWOC's "organizing." Most contractors in the northern end of the San Joaquin Valley— over a hundred of them—eventually signed "contracts" with AWOC. Under these agreements, they deducted a month's dues (two dollars) from each worker's pay each day, up to a maximum of twelve months in advance.

Almost everybody was happy. Growers were relieved of any necessity to recognize a union. Labor contractors continued to make their profits. AWOC gathered substantial numbers of "members" without effort. George Meany was delighted that AWOC had at last been put on a sound, businesslike basis. Urban liberals slept well, with the thought that the farm labor movement was again in competent professional hands.

The "members"? Apparently they did not object to paying for a kind of ticket which guaranteed them admission to a bus without any unpleasantness. Some were no doubt oblivious to the whole business.

Almost everybody was happy—except bona fide farm laborers and bona fide farm labor organizers. Cesar Chavez, who by this time had begun organizing on his own in Delano, was appalled. He said, "I would rather that there be no union at all than to recognize the rotten contractor system."

Norman Smith stayed with AWOC until his retirement in 1964. The organization always bore the imprint he had put upon it. He had not lacked advice which would have produced a totally different type of AWOC. From his first visit to Stockton, in early May, 1959, he had had the benefit of counsel from several of the same persons who most profoundly influenced Chavez and the Delano movement which was to come: Fred Ross and Dolores Huerta of the Community Service Organization; Fathers McCullough, McDonnell, and Ralph Duggan. All of them said the same things: concentrate on the home guard; organize around the felt needs of the people; let them choose their own spokesmen; don't be maneuvered into premature strikes. If Smith had followed their advice, AWOC could probably have built by September, 1960, with the level of resources it enjoyed, the same kind of infrastructure that it took Chavez, working by himself, until September, 1965, to build. Smith rejected all their advice—or rather, he was not really able to hear what they were saying—and five years of the farm labor movement were lost.

AWOC was not totally without accomplishments. Before government agencies learned that there were no teeth behind its barking, AWOC had some effect in reducing the numbers of braceros authorized for California. This fact, coupled with the efforts of the self-organized fruit tramps, produced a rise in wages, particularly in orchard crops. At the end of the 1960 season, AWOC's Director of Research estimated that this increase had been in the neighborhood of $20 million altogether, although this estimate gave AWOC the benefit of most doubts.

With its resources, AWOC was able to send spokesmen around the country, testifying at legislative hearings and speaking at conventions. The level of public awareness was raised. The farm labor movement took several more steps up from anonymity. Although Smith and

Agribusiness in California is a big, highly mechanized industry. *Right,* a mechanical cotton harvester. Farms average about seven hundred acres in size, nearly double the national average, and tend to be unusually productive due to intensive irrigation, *below,* and use of artificial fertilizers and pesticides. (ERNEST LOWE)

Farm labor conditions in California are "good" compared to those in many other parts of the country. *Above,* a "shoestring community" in Fresno County; *right,* a ditch-bank camp in Stanislaus County. (GEORGE BALLIS and ERNEST LOWE)

The 4:30 A.M. shape-up in Stockton, scene of organizing efforts by the Agricultural Workers Organizing Committee. Although they now form only a small part of the California farm labor force, single male transients have worked in the fields since the 1850's when disappointed gold seekers began turning to agriculture. (GEORGE BALLIS)

Despite federal and state laws, child labor is still commonplace in California fields. *Right,* six-to-eight-year-olds top carrots in "Steinbeck Country" near Salinas. (ERNEST LOWE)

Much of California agriculture still depends on skilled hand labor. No machine can select, cut, and trim the table grapes grown in the Delano area, *below*. (GEORGE BALLIS)

A pioneer in the farm labor movement, Father Thomas McCullough, the *bracero* priest, addressing the Agricultural Workers Organizing Conference, Strathmore, 1961. (ERNEST LOWE)

Dolores Huerta, vice-president of United Farm Workers Organizing Committee, mother of seven, has been demonstrating for nearly fifteen years that woman's place may be in *la causa* as well as *la casa*. (GEORGE BALLIS)

Fred Van Dyke, *top left,* the farmer driven out of farming because of his support for the agricultural workers' movement; Ernesto Galarza, *bottom left,* only doctor of philosophy ever elected to office in a national union; and Larry Itliong, *below,* Filipino community leader and assistant director, United Farm Workers Organizing Committee. (HENRY ANDERSON, GEORGE BALLIS, and HENRY ANDERSON)

Cesar Chavez's aim is to build a union which is a true community of human beings, not just an economic vending machine. At countless house meetings, 1962–1965, he laid a foundation by explaining to farm laborers what they could accomplish by working together. (GEORGE BALLIS)

Above, Epifanio Camacho, picket captain for the National Farm Workers Association, after the grape strike began in September, 1965. Sign on the flag means, "Scab, come out." *Below,* pickets protest the welfare department's "work or starve" order in Salinas Valley. (GEORGE BALLIS)

El Teatro Campesino, or Farm Workers Theater, is one of the union's many innovations. Here Luís Valdez, founder of the *teatro,* plays the role of "Don Coyote," a farm labor contractor, and Augustín Lira mimes a credulous farm worker. (GEORGE BALLIS)

La Peregrinación, a 230-mile, 25-day march from Delano to the State Capitol in Sacramento in 1966, was a public relations triumph for the grape strikers. *Above,* the pilgrimage passes a field of winter wheat. *Below,* the rally which concluded the march on Easter Sunday. (BART ABBOTT and GEORGE BALLIS)

Chavez limps with blistered feet in la peregrinación. (GEORGE BALLIS)

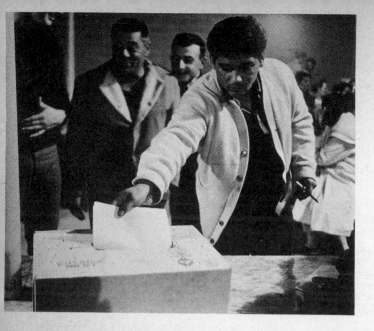

After winning a contract at the Gallo vineyards, members of the UFWOC vote for stewards to represent them in maintaining the contract, *above*. UFWOC meetings traditionally conclude with members' joining hands, *below*, and singing "Nosotros Venceremos" (We Shall Overcome). (GEORGE BALLIS)

The grape strikers and boycotters received valuable aid from many national figures. Just before Christmas, 1965, Walter Reuther, *right,* came to Delano to pledge $5,000 a month support from his United Automobile Workers Union. In March, 1966, Sen. Robert F. Kennedy, *below,* lent his prestige to the movement. (GEORGE BALLIS)

Helen Chavez, Sen. Robert F. Kennedy, and Cesar Chavez praying together in Delano in March, 1968, following Chavez's Lenten fast during which he rededicated himself to the principle of nonviolent direct action. (GEORGE BALLIS)

Galarza were by far the best-known names, others on the initial AWOC staff included Dolores Huerta, Henry Anderson, Louis Krainock, Andy Arellano, Cipriano (Rudy) Delvo, Art Cooper, Raul Aguilar, and Vance Ambrose. Organizers added later included George Seratt, Maria Moreno, and Larry Itliong.

All the major California newspapers sent reporters to Stockton to get the inside story on labor's "big push" in agriculture (and every one managed to miss the important story, on organizing strategy). Many national magazines carried articles. The CBS television network did a documentary, "Harvest of Shame," narrated by Edward R. Murrow, which prominently featured AWOC.

But all these were peripheral to the point of union-building, which is to organize people into lasting structures. This, AWOC never did, although it spent far more money than any organizing drive in American agriculture, before or since: well over a million dollars in all. It was bankrupted by too much money, in the sense that money was used as a substitute for intelligence. The most basic of the several misconceptions at work in AFL-CIO upper echelons, throughout the history of AWOC, was the assumption that money is the answer to all organizing problems; that one did not need a rational plan; if only the right amount of money were spent, farm workers would automatically fall into line. In its own way, this attitude was as paternalistic and contemptuous of farm workers as the attitude of growers. And it killed AWOC.

Many conclusions might be drawn from the struggles of California farm workers to redress what they have perceived as unfair imbalances between themselves and their employers. One, perhaps, is outstanding. Organization by agricultural workers is unlike the organization of any other kind of workers, in the amount of deprivation it exacts.

Lacking even the rudiments of orderly machinery for the resolution of differences with growers, and given the fact that growers have declined to concede the existence of farm labor unions, much less their right to exist, agricultural workers have had no alternative to striking in support of their demands. A strike is the last extremity for any group of employees, for it cuts them off from their livelihood. But a farm labor strike is more demanding than any other. Farm workers do not have personal savings to call upon; their unions have never had strike benefit funds; and, unlike most other types of workers, farm laborers cannot make up their lost wages by overtime, filling back orders, after the strike is over.

Yet large numbers of California farm laborers have on many occasions foregone an entire season's income—sometimes several seasons' income—in strikes they must have known they did not have a chance in a hundred of winning. Why?

Evidently the farm labor movement speaks to something fundamental in the needs of agricultural workers, something which they share, perhaps, with all men. The need seems to be more psychological than material, which suggests that the movement will go on, in the face of starvation, or jail—or even if agricultural employers were suddenly to upgrade wages and working conditions out of enlightened self-interest.

The fundamental human need to which the farm labor movement speaks is the need to feel one has exercised some degree of control over one's life, has accomplished something difficult and honorable through one's efforts, working together in a common cause with compatriots who are making the same kinds of sacrifices. Among other types of people, this means other forms of self-organization and self-renunciation. Among agricultural workers, it means but one thing: to build a union.

4. God's Laughing Man: Father Thomas McCullough

During the greater part of the 1950's, an organizational vacuum existed in most of the agricultural regions of California. The area around Stockton, however, was an exception. There, a young Catholic priest, in addition to ecclesiastical duties in his largely Mexican-American parish, functioned with rare effectiveness as an organizer of farm workers.

To his unsought task, Father Thomas McCullough brought personal qualities so various, and at times even contradictory, as to confound all the neat theories of how leaders function in social movements. He had a rare grasp of the whole agricultural labor problem, yet was happy to drop from view in the most mundane, plodding duties; he was at once an inspiring leader and the most faithful of followers; he could be now a dreamer, now the most tough-minded of men. Above all, Father McCullough confounded those who believe a social movement must be made up of grim-lipped zealots. He brought to everything he did, to all with whom he spoke and worked, a rare gift of laughter—a generous, spontaneous laughter which blunted the edges of bitterness and loss, lightened despair, disarmed opponents, and rekindled enthusiasm in followers as they found their failures did not usher in a *Dies Irae*.

Grandfather McCullough came from Ireland. He tried farming in Illinois for a time. Then, because construction work was less subject to vagaries of the economy, he entered the building trades and insisted that each of his seven sons also learn a trade.

In 1910, the entire clan moved to the San Francisco Bay area. Since the city was still rebuilding after the great earthquake and fire of 1906, construction work was plentiful. The McCulloughs purchased a lot in Albany, on the east side of the bay. The father and his sons built a large house for the family. During World War I, several of the McCullough boys served in the army, including the eldest, Thomas

Patrick. In Europe, he met and fell in love with a Belgian girl, Anna Mertins, whom he married when the war was over. In accordance with Irish tradition, the eldest son and his bride moved into the family home, and when Grandfather McCullough died, Thomas Patrick became head of the clan.

A son, Thomas Aloysius McCullough, was born to Thomas Patrick and Anna in 1922. The fact that he was raised in the family seat influenced the boy in important ways. Almost every evening, one or more of the McCullough brothers stopped to visit. Much discussion revolved around the subject of unionism. During the 1930's, the building trades unions of the East Bay were trying to obtain union shop contracts. Thomas Patrick McCullough, a member of the Bricklayers and Stonemasons, believed staunchly in unions. Some of his brothers, however, did not, and on occasion worked as strikebreakers. Thomas Aloysius later recalled: "Some of my earliest memories are the knock-down-and-drag-out arguments there used to be in the kitchen. . . . [Somebody] let the union down, saying that he had a wife and children to support. My father forbade us ever to go to his house again."

Thomas Patrick McCullough also had a wife and children to support—in time, two sons and two daughters—but even in the depths of the Depression, he never "let the union down." When necessary to avoid strikebreaking, he traveled far afield to find work, and was sometimes separated from his family for months. When work outside the Bay Area grew scarce, he mortgaged the family home, and eventually lost it when he could not meet the payments. In view of the symbolic significance of the home to the entire McCullough clan, this was a sacrifice beyond monetary calculation.

Young Thomas did not master the legal and moral theories of unionism until later, but by the time he was eight or ten years old, he had learned a more basic lesson: that there would be no union without great selflessness and suffering on the part of at least some of the workers. From observation of his own uncles, he anticipated that some workers would hold back, risk nothing, and then enjoy the benefits of unionism after it was an accomplished fact. But he knew that someone would have to risk everything. At some deep level, he was convinced that unions were established only through spiritual, almost explicitly Christian means: the salvation of all achieved through the agony of a few.

Another important influence upon Thomas McCullough appeared in his life nearly as early. When he was six, he entered a parochial school in Berkeley. One of his classmates was Donald McDonnell. As the years went by and other boyhood friendships faded, theirs grew stronger. By the time they were in the eighth grade, both had decided to make a vocation of the priesthood.

For preparatory work they went to St. Joseph's College in the Santa Clara Valley. During one summer vacation, McCullough did farm work in the valley, picking and cutting apricots. "I averaged between ten and fifteen cents an hour," he recalled, years later.

After four years at St. Joseph's, McCullough and McDonnell went to St. Patrick's Seminary in Menlo Park for the six years of additional college work required for ordination. Father Joseph Munier's course on social justice provided a systematic introduction to the papal encyclicals on the economic order: *Rerum novarum* (Pope Leo XIII, 1891) and *Quadragessimo anno* (Pope Pius XI, 1931). For most of the seminarians, it was a revelation to learn that "workingmen's associations" were held by the most authoritative teachings of the Church to be consonant with Natural Law; hence, workers had not only a right to join unions but a moral duty. It was also a revelation to learn that, on occasion, priests—such as Father Peter Yorke of San Francisco around the turn of the century—had actively engaged in union organizing with the full knowledge and consent of their bishops.

Forty-five minutes were set aside each day for recreation at St. Patrick's, but at McDonnell's suggestion several of the seminarians used this time to conduct "a seminar within a seminary." The informal group included Ralph Duggan, John Garcia, and Ronald Burke, besides McCullough and McDonnell. They taught themselves Spanish while strolling through the seminary gardens every evening after supper. Late at night, after three hours of obligatory study, they often discussed contemporary developments within Catholicism, such as the Catholic Worker movement in New York City, led by Peter Maurin and Dorothy Day. There was no talk of a "new breed" of priests. McCullough, McDonnell, and the others considered themselves totally loyal to the traditional Church and its teachings. Their studies convinced them that that loyalty required, among other things, a devotion to social justice.

They were ordained in 1947; they took their vows of poverty, chastity, and obedience; they scattered to begin apprenticeships as assistant parish priests. McCullough was assigned to "Old St. Mary's" in downtown Stockton.

Father Thomas McCullough: a dignified title which seemed a little strange when applied to the young man who looked even younger than his twenty-four years. He was nearly six feet tall, muscular, his hair light brown and slightly wavy, his eyes hazel, his features handsome. He was quite capable of seriousness; he knew anger and grief; but he never forgot that there was joy in being alive, in being human, in being a priest, in doing God's work.

Father McCullough's first duties in Stockton involved working with children and youth. A strike of Filipino asparagus workers was in progress in the area, but McCullough did not become associated with it. His baptism in the farm labor river took place slowly and almost unnoticed. In the late fall of 1947, he was assigned to a parish survey in the fringes of Stockton, the terra incognita of the local church. Nothing in his seminary studies had prepared the young priest for this task. The large numbers of Mexican nationals he encountered spoke no English; his Spanish was still far from adequate. And he discovered that most of the questions he was supposed to ask were irrelevant. What could he ask wetbacks, housed in uncleaned chicken coops, about the exercise of their faith? If they went to town for confession or mass, they were subject to arrest and deportation. The accepted Catholic precepts did not apply.

This gradual introduction to farm labor proved important to Father McCullough and to the movement he was later to join. Going into the field without preconceptions, McCullough was able to see it as a complicated mixture of human frailties and contradictions. Eventually, he made judgments as to where the balance lay and the kinds of action demanded of the just man, but he never lent himself to simple dichotomies, sweeping generalizations, or sentimentality. In considerable measure, his successes to come were the result of his freedom from illusion: the illusion, for instance, that agricultural workers are especially saintly, or agricultural employers especially savage.

Father McCullough's early census-taking experience also marked his first use of a basic method for making contact with strangers: the door-to-door method, in which one overcomes the initial gap by the spark of personal recognition and response. McCullough remembered it in later years when questions arose about building a farm labor union. He was always skeptical of crowd techniques: appeals by handbill, sound truck, newspaper, radio, or other means to lure workers to rallies consisting of hortatory speeches by unknown "leaders."

For two and a half years, Father McCullough worked quietly, growing closer to the people in the Stockton area, many of them agricultural workers, some of them agricultural employers, learning more about the problems and thinking more about the possible answers.

Early in June, 1950, he and Father Donald McDonnell called at the chancery office of the San Francisco archdiocese and placed before Archbishop John J. Mitty a proposal. They asked to be relieved of ordinary parish assignments in order to function as "priests to the poor" throughout the diocese, which then covered thirteen northern California counties. They pointed out that in rural counties the Church was serving Italian and Portuguese growers who made generous contributions, but was largely failing to serve those who were unable to contribute financially: tens of thousands of Spanish-speaking people, most of them farm workers.

With minor modifications, the proposal was accepted. Fathers McCullough, McDonnell, John Garcia, and Ronald Burke were assigned to what was called the Spanish Mission Band, later known as the Missionary Apostolate.

These four, none of them yet thirty, went forth to deal with a population of at least 100,000 rural poor, to be supplemented within a few years by at least 35,000 to 40,000 foreign contract workers. Before they were done, these four priests, McCullough and McDonnell in particular, were unable to avoid confrontations with the power structure of California agribusiness, government agencies, major segments of organized labor, and sections of their own church.

Father McDonnell's home base became a Mexican *colónia* in San Jose; Father McCullough's was St. Gertrude's parish in Stockton. McCullough's territory included all of San Joaquin and Stanislaus counties and the eastern portion of Contra Costa County. This territory contained at least a thousand farm labor camps known to the state Division of Housing, and untold numbers of ditch-bank and chicken-coop camps ignored by the authorities.

Two months after the Mission Band started, Ernesto Galarza and Hank Hasiwar, representing the National Farm Labor Union, began to organize the tomato pickers of the Tracy area, about twenty miles southwest of Stockton. It was McCullough's first direct encounter with farm labor organizing. McDonnell joined him almost every night. Together, they talked to the different types of workers in the area. Some camps were for wetbacks only; some for braceros. There were still many family camps at that time—local tomato workers had not yet been wholly displaced by braceros.

Some of the camps catered to all three types of workers. One was located alongside the Tracy dump. Mexicans are fond of ironic nicknames for persons, objects, and places. They had dubbed this miserable camp Angeles de Dios (the Angels of God). Of this camp, McCullough recalled:

"The [braceros] were deeply troubled. They had made great sacrifices to come to this country; I knew that. They had families back in Mexico, most of them; I knew that. So it wasn't an easy thing. They came to me and said, 'Padre, what should we do? This strike . . . is it good?' I just talked with them about their rights under the Natural Law to band together with other workers, and things like that. And then I remember, very distinctly, the operator of the camp came around. He saw the men sitting there, and he frowned, and he said—I can remember his exact words—'*Al trabajo o a México!*' (To work or to Mexico!) The men looked at me, and at him, and they said, '*A México!*' And that was that. Back they went, making wry fun of themselves the way Mexicans do when they are unhappy."

Out of such experiences, Father McCullough's misgivings about the foreign labor system grew, and his concepts of organizing methods began to take form. That he would one day be making strategic decisions, however, did not occur to him. For seven more years, he took for granted that the responsibility for organizing farm workers belonged to the labor movement, and that his own responsibility was to inform workers of the Church's teachings on social justice.

After Public Law 78 was enacted in 1951, and the numbers of braceros imported into California increased geometrically, Fathers McCullough and McDonnell became known as the "bracero priests," or "padres." They did not neglect the local Spanish-speaking poor, but braceros were even less likely to be reached by the regular services of the Church, and were therefore particularly in need of the unique services of the Mission Band. McCullough sometimes found himself in embarrassing situations. More than once, he entered a bracero barrack late in the evening or early in the morning to be told, "You must come back later to say mass, padre. There are girls here now." Although he was able to laugh at the way he must have appeared in such circumstances, he was not able to laugh at the bracero system itself. Invariably patient with individual human failings, he had no patience with a system which preyed on such failings and aggravated them.

As part of God's law, he argued, a man has a right to a family, and within the family, duties to his wife as a husband and to his children as a father. Exceptions might be made for the man who voluntarily relinquishes his natural right in order to become a priest, and for those who respond to a genuine national emergency and temporarily renounce family life in the interests of defending their country. There were no such justifications for the sundering of families under the bracero system. As Father McCullough put it:

". . . here is a system that sets up a special caste. It affects *only* agricultural workers who come from Mexico or some other foreign country. It doesn't give them a choice whether they want to bring their families with them or not. If they had any choice, they would like to bring their families—almost all of them. I've talked to hundreds . . . thousands. But they've got to sacrifice all of that—just so we can get our food picked, cheap.

"It is a purely selfish purpose. The Church has a lot of complicated theology about justifying things when there is an overriding purpose. You've heard of the idea of a just war? Well, there's nothing like that here. . . . It's purely selfish. And so I think we have to say that it is morally evil."

Father McCullough questioned the practice, employed by some critics of the bracero system, of trying to move government officials, organized labor, and the general public by "horror stories." For instance, McCullough knew a man and his wife and children who arrived in Stockton in 1956, toward the very end of onion-sacking—at best, a notoriously low-paying job—and for the rest of the season were able to average only about three cents per person per hour. But McCullough made no public use of this or similar stories, for he had learned that they were likely to prove a distraction. They were usually countered by a cherry or peach grower who claimed some of his workers made $30 or more in a day. McCullough knew that such comparatively princely earnings doubtless represented a whole family "picking into the same bucket," but how could one prove that? And without access to growers' payrolls (assuming such records existed at all) how could one prove one's "horror stories"?

McCullough had seen the man-in-the-street, legislators, and others bombarded by extreme claims from worker and grower partisans throw up their hands and decline to get involved at all. He therefore advised a calm, understated approach, and followed it himself.

"I try to just talk about the normal, the average. Any decent person with common sense will know that is bad enough. Do the growers say the average wage is 90 cents an hour? All right, use that. Joe Doaks will know that you can't support a family on 90 cents an hour. Do the growers set the wage in tomatoes at 11 cents a box? All right, use that. A box is 50 pounds, minimum. That is about one-fifth of a penny a pound. Joe will get the point. He knows that tomatoes cost 20 or 25 cents a pound in the market."

During the bracero season, which ran from February to December in Father McCullough's part of California, he went to a bracero camp almost every night. In 1956, for example, he visited 260 camps and saw at least 10,000 braceros: an actual head-count of men who attended his bunkhouse masses. After mass he talked with most of them personally.

There was probably never anyone with a more intimate knowledge of the actual workings of braceroism, gained from the lives of the men themselves, than Father McCullough. For the most part, he used this knowledge only to attack the system as a whole. He was well aware that his energies could easily become totally diverted if he let himself be cast in the role of compliance officer, enforcing the terms of Public Law 78, defending the rights of individual braceros. Only occasionally did he encounter an abuse so outrageous that he threw his unexampled energy into the case, writing or telephoning the Mexican consul, the governor of California, or the man with ultimate authority over the bracero system, the Secretary of Labor.

As if his duties were not already heavy enough, in 1956 Father McCullough began to build a church, in every spiritual, sociological, and physical sense of those words. Many seasonal farm laborers lived in an unincorporated area of South Stockton. The people there were strangers to one another; there was no community. McCullough, using his house-to-house technique, began building a sense of community first, and then, with almost all of the work being done by his congregation and himself, St. Linus Mission began to rise. The area, for years lacking an identity, became popularly known as the "St. Linus District," and is known as such to this day.

From that point on, Father McCullough was not only priest to tens of thousands of braceros; he was also a parish priest, officiating at masses, hearing confessions, instructing young people who wanted to be married, visiting the afflicted in hospitals and jails, and performing a hundred other duties. He had to worry about mortgage payments; he had to conduct bazaars and other fund-raising functions; he was appointed to a Community Welfare Council. He did it all gladly, for he was growing increasingly certain that the solution to the bracero problem lay in the organization of domestic agricultural workers.

Father McCullough remembers with a smile that he was originally considered the "incorrigible idealist" of the Mission Band, but his idealism was tempered as time went by. In his encounters with the officialdom of the bracero system—growers, Farm Placement Service agents, labor contractors, and the minor functionaries he sometimes called "camp followers"—he returned with increasing frequency and certainty to a lesson he had first heard from his father in family discussions around the kitchen stove in Albany: an individual, however great his moral purity, intellectual force, skill with words, or other personal qualities, counts for little in a changing society unless he has a power base.

McCullough tended less and less to write letters to editors or undertake other projects on his own. He and McDonnell became regional spokesmen for the National Catholic Rural Life Conference, an organization dedicated to applying Catholic principles to life on the land. Nationally, its principal concern had long been the preservation of the family farm; it had been dormant in California for some time. When lawmakers asked at a public hearing, "Is this an official organization?" it gave Father McCullough visible satisfaction to be able to answer, "Yes, sir. An official arm of the Church in America." It was not as easy to ignore a witness with such credentials as it was to brush aside a lone priest who was speaking for no one but himself.

McCullough never felt at home in the political process as he did in bracero camps and shoestring community house meetings. So long as he believed it would speed the day of agricultural organization, however, he took part in the political process. Both he and Father McDonnell testified before many congressional and state legislative committees. In 1960, for instance, they prepared a piece of testimony which was approved by the Bishop of Sacramento, Joseph T. McGucken, now Archbishop of San Francisco. It contained several of the themes about which the two priests felt most strongly:

> The most obvious solution of the problem of farm labor is that farm work should be done by farmers. Public policy should safeguard our state and nation against the dangers of collectivism either by government socialism or private monopoly. Legislation should strongly encourage . . . real farmers [to work] together in true Rochdale cooperatives . . . constituting an up-to-date rural society which would bring to the people of the land all the benefits of 20th century progress.

> Facing realistically, however, the . . . pressure of vertical integration both on working farmers and farm workers, it is clear that the . . . imperative need [is for] farm employers and farm workers . . . with the aid of government, to set up the indispensable machinery for stable and just labor-management relations. This . . . means organization of workers into unions . . . to get from the whole economy the proper recompense for the agricultural industry.

McCullough's mature judgment was reached after years of immersion in the agricultural labor situation: a peculiarly intimate immersion because, as a priest, he heard things not generally revealed to others; and a total immersion because, as a celibate, without family obligations, he was able to devote himself eighteen hours a day, or more, to his mission. His seasoned judgment was that the bracero problem, "labor shortages," wages, housing, health, education, child labor, all the many vexing facets of the agricultural labor problem, were symptomatic; that, at its core, it was a labor-management problem. Hence, priests and lawyers and legislators and others could not solve it, but at best could only assist agricultural employees and employers to solve it through negotiating collectively between themselves.

Father McCullough was far from insensitive to the position of farmers. In the middle 1950's, he spent a great deal of time trying to talk with farmers about constructive solutions to the disorganized state of their industry. If he had received any encouragement, he might have devoted himself to helping farmers organize buying and marketing cooperatives, and the history of the farm labor movement would then have been different. Receiving no encouragement, he was forced to the same conclusion that other farm labor moderates have reached sooner or later: growers will not take constructive steps until they are required to, and the only power which can require them to do so is the power of their organized workers.

Among friends of the farm labor movement, Father McCullough's energy became legendary. Nightly, he visited bracero camps; daily, he continued to build St. Linus Mission. To keep in personal touch with the realities of farm labor, he worked in the fields from time to time. "Thinning sugar beets with that short-handled hoe really gets you in the back of the legs," he said ruefully. And, somehow, he managed to appear at virtually all the farm labor conferences held during the 1950's—and there were dozens. Every liberal group in the country, it seemed, held a conference or workshop or seminar on "the plight of the migrant," heard both sides, decided that the workers had the better of the argument, passed a resolution to that effect, and adjourned.

Distances to be covered and the scant time left from McCullough's and McDonnell's local duties led to an evolution in their means of transportation. They began with a Volkswagen microbus, well suited to the back roads of the San Joaquin Delta. McCullough carried as many as sixteen braceros in his blue microbus. But on one occasion, the two padres wanted to attend a conference in Texas and needed to get there and back in four days. They bought a motorcycle, and drove at 70 miles an hour, nonstop except for refueling, taking turns at the handlebars; the passenger slept, lashed to the driver with a rope.

Even this did not meet the need of the padres to be many places at once. They bought an airplane: an old TriPacer, which they overhauled themselves. Father McCullough eventually became a licensed pilot. He had at least three close brushes with death, but laughed at them as just another joke on himself, no more serious than the time a particularly husky grower threw him bodily down the stairs of a bracero barrack.

Even the most knowledgeable friends of the farm labor movement were rarely aware of how heavily McCullough and McDonnell were paying for their lavish expenditures of time and energy. After the secular meetings were done, and everyone else went home to sleep, the priests still had to "say their office": devotions in Latin, requiring close to an hour. When they were together, they were able to finish— by slapping each other's faces to stay awake, if necessary. But when they were alone, it was more difficult. Sometimes Father McCullough collapsed before he was through. A parishioner might find him the next morning, slumped where he had fallen.

On the assumption that organizing the unorganized was the proper responsibility of existing unions, Fathers McDonnell and McCullough stormed the citadels of the labor movement, trying to make leaders face up to their responsibilities. To finance these travels about the country, the priests incurred personal debts they were still repaying many years later. They talked to Ralph Helstein, head of the Packinghouse Workers, who said that his union had "plans," but the time was not quite ripe. They talked to Patrick Gorman, head of the Meatcutters, who said he had heard there were "Communists in the thing in California." They talked to Teamster officials, without results. They talked to leaders of the International Longshoremen's and Warehousemen's Union, who had organized agriculture in Hawaii, but who lacked funds and staff for an expansion into California's plantations.

They talked to George Meany, who, although a Catholic himself, found it incomprehensible that a priest would travel three thousand miles to talk to him about farm labor. "But, Father," he asked in bewilderment, "what do *you* have to do with it?" In the end, he advised them to talk to C. J. Haggerty, executive secretary-treasurer of the California Labor Federation, who, Meany thought, could spare some money for farm labor organizing. When they saw Haggerty, the best he would do was place the Federation's research department "at their disposal." But when they talked to Jack Henning, the Federation's director of research (later U.S. Undersecretary of Labor, and ambassador to New Zealand; now Haggerty's successor as head of the Federation) he asked them to tell *him* what was going on in agriculture in California.

In 1958, Father McCullough reached the final step in the logical progression he had been following. If none of the organizations which should be doing the job could or would do it, and if he were truly serious in his conviction that farm workers had to be organized, there seemed only one conclusion. Father McCullough became an organizer of farm workers himself.

The timing was providential. At almost the same moment, Fred Ross, of the Community Service Organization, arrived in Stockton. Although the CSO was not, strictly speaking, a farm labor organization, its organizing assumptions and techniques were almost identical to the conclusions reached independently by Father McCullough. McCullough introduced to the CSO one of his parishioners, a young woman named Dolores Huerta, who was to be among his most telling legacies to the farm labor movement. In time, she became principal lieutenant to Cesar Chavez.

One of the first steps in McCullough's organizing process was to find a farm worker willing to hold a meeting in his house and guarantee that at least half a dozen other agricultural workers, whom he knew personally, would be there. At this initial meeting, an attempt was made to find two more persons willing to hold meetings in their own homes, and at those meetings still other volunteers.

It was a process of growth by "cellular division" which McCullough, grinning mischievously, admitted had been used by "the Communist Party, the Nazis, and others who weren't very nice." But, breaking into laughter, he went on to point out, "It was also used by the Church in its early days."

By November, 1958, house meetings were being held every night of the week. Discussions frequently lasted until long past midnight.

This was the start of the period when, the tomato harvest being virtually completed and winter pruning not yet begun, San Joaquin County farm workers had plenty of time to talk.

What did they talk about? McCullough recalled:

"We had no fixed agenda. The important thing was to get people to know each other, and find out the interests and problems they had in common. Out of this would come mutual respect and trust. I remember one of the things that came out. When you let farm workers just talk, you learn that they see nothing intrinsically wrong with farm work, nothing degrading, nothing to be ashamed of. On the contrary, they feel it is good, useful work. In this, they can find honor for themselves: 'The work is honorable, therefore we are honorable men.' This is very important. If farm workers get the idea they deserve to be a separate, low-grade caste, then you're going to have a tough time getting them to make demands on society.

"One of the things we didn't talk about was strike, which would have either scared people off or raised false expectations.

". . . I got a pretty good idea of what they'd think of when they heard the word 'union'—something mechanical, like a train heading down the tracks. You bought your ticket—your dues—got on board, and it would take you where you wanted to go. This came from seeing the way established unions work, without having the slightest idea of the suffering they had gone through to get to that point.

"To get away from wrong impressions, we used the word 'association'—an Agricultural Workers Association—to describe what we were trying to do. Just to get farm workers associating with one another was the main thing, the first thing, to do."

Under McCullough's organizational model, those who attended the small meetings were also supposed to attend weekly general meetings in order to exchange views on what they had been discussing, and to identify areas of common agreement and potential action. It proved difficult to follow this model. Rumors about the Agricultural Workers Association were spreading swiftly among farm workers of the area. Many who had not been to house meetings, and therefore lacked any background for decision-making, appeared at the first general meeting. The large attendance was gratifying, but precluded the kind of discussion McCullough had visualized. A second general meeting, held in the recreation hall of Old St. Mary's in downtown Stockton, attracted even more hundreds of people: the audience overflowed into the lobby and out into the street. At such a mass meeting, a few people make speeches, while the overwhelming majority silently listen, with no one speaking directly for them.

Mrs. Huerta, Father McCullough, and others on a de facto AWA steering committee took stock. They decided to hold the general meetings monthly instead of weekly, and to re-emphasize the importance of attending at least one house meeting before the larger meetings. They agreed that some kind of agenda, shaped by subjects discussed at the smaller meetings, was necessary. Finally, it was agreed that each of the smaller groups would have a spokesman, and that in the course of the larger meeting every spokesman would be called upon to speak for his group.

The house meetings continued to spread. People who were not among McCullough's parishioners, who had no connection with the CSO, who were neither Catholic nor Spanish-speaking, began to volunteer: Cipriano Delvo of the Filipino community, for instance, and North Hayes, a Negro minister who was also a farm worker.

A general meeting in January, 1959, went so well that an acting board of directors was elected, with the framing of a constitution its immediate task. By February, several hundred workers were attending house meetings and had subscribed to the constitution. Its preamble read:

We, the men and women voluntarily associating ourselves as members of this non-profit organization, do so recognizing:

1) That God gave the earth to man for his needs and that man by his labor and skill yields wealth from the earth.

2) That this wealth does not belong exclusively to capital; nor does it belong exclusively to labor; rather, that there must be a just distribution according to the common good, with cooperation between capital and labor.

3) That man has the right to organize and adopt such rules of organization as are in keeping with justice and the common welfare . . . WHEREFORE, the purpose of this association is, by mutual effort, to help each and every agricultural worker to better his condition in body and soul and property—receiving a just distribution of the wealth he produces from the soil.

Planning proceeded. Members of the AWA were ready to pay monthly dues as soon as a dues structure was agreed upon; an executive secretary, willing to work for $200 a month, was recruited; a system of committees was worked out. According to the plan, every AWA member, in order to remain in good standing, was supposed to work actively on at least one of the following committees: membership, finance, employment, social and educational activities, housing, health and welfare, political action, community service and mutual aid.

The ferment included some remarkably refreshing ideas. For example, Father McCullough advanced the notion of a "reverse strike," similar to a concept Danilo Dolci was putting into effect in Sicily, although at the time McCullough had never heard of Dolci. Thousands of local farm laborers in the Stockton area wanted to work but could not find work because they had been displaced by braceros. To make themselves more highly visible to the community as a whole, and to make it clear that they were perfectly able and willing to perform the kinds of tasks found in agriculture, McCullough proposed that they form crews to clear weeds from the sides of roads and the like.

When this idea was broached at an AWA meeting, someone rose to ask, "Since there would be no pay for this work, how would we live?" Someone else shot back, "How are we living now?" The idea of a "reverse strike" was adopted as one of the techniques to be employed by AWA during the next big influx of braceros.

Some of the planning for AWA's mutual aid committee called for nothing less than a sociological, economic, and psychological community of agricultural workers, resembling a kibbutz, except that members would continue to live in private dwellings, often quite dispersed geographically. The cooperative buying of food, clothing and other essentials, and the sharing of skills was envisioned. It was anticipated that produce would be grown on several acres of undeveloped land in back of St. Linus Mission.

One may conjecture what might have happened in the farm labor movement, and perhaps in broader currents of social change in the United States, if the joy, energy, and organizing skill of Father Thomas McCullough had continued being directed toward visions such as these. But developments across the continent cut short his plans.

When the creation of an Agricultural Workers Organizing Committee was announced in February, 1959, Father McCullough thought this entry of the AFL-CIO into the field represented the breakthrough he had sought for so long. With the best of will and highest of hopes, he and Father McDonnell, at the invitation of Jack Livingston, AFL-CIO director of organization joined Ernesto Galarza, H. L. Mitchell, and others at a planning session in San Francisco in March, 1959.

There can be no doubt that the decision to place AWOC headquarters in Stockton was made because Father McCullough and his co-workers had already organized the Agricultural Workers Association there. McCullough had every reason to expect that AWOC would continue to build on the same foundation and with the same techniques.

In April, Norman Smith was picked as director of AWOC: he spoke at the AWA general meeting the following month. He had already rented office space and started to hire staff. There seemed no point, and, indeed, positive danger in continuing a parallel, independent existence for AWA. At its June meeting, without audible dissent, the AWA membership voted to dissolve in favor of AWOC. Nothing more was ever heard of the organization which Father McCullough had begun so well—although, three years later, something strikingly similar was to appear in the little town of Delano, two hundred miles to the south, under the leadership of Cesar Chavez.

If Thomas McCullough, a man of parts, has a vulnerable part it was revealed in the period from June, 1959, to June, 1961. Everything he had built, and the methods he had used, were disregarded while he watched and kept his own counsel. His convictions about the necessity for "team play" overrode his convictions about the best way to organize agricultural workers.

Norman Smith was well aware of McCullough's accomplishments. He respected the man and his works. There was never any question of jealousy; there was, indeed, a good deal of personal affection between the two. But Smith never really accepted, apparently because he never really understood, the McCullough-CSO approach to organizing.

The McCullough-CSO organizing model rested on local workers with wives and children, with permanent residences, with highly developed skills in agricultural tasks, prepared to make a permanent career of farm work if only they could earn a tolerable living at it. These workers were in the most pivotal positions to influence the productivity of the industry. They did the pruning, spraying, cultivating, irrigating, and other tasks without which there would be no crops to harvest. They also did most of the harvesting. Contrary to popular assumption, relatively few California farm workers were migrants, and the proportion was growing smaller as more of them settled in shoestring communities and tried to eke out a livelihood within a radius of forty or fifty miles. Of the total man-days which go into California agriculture each year, probably not more than 10 or 12 percent are supplied by either interstate or intrastate migrants.

Before AWA bowed out of existence in favor of AWOC, Smith attended a few of McCullough's house meetings with the Stockton home guard. No one was pleased. AWA members, accustomed to give-and-take in their organization, were not greatly charmed by a man whose idea of a meeting was a two-hour speech by himself. For his part, Smith was baffled when his best anecdotes about organizing automobile workers in the 1930's failed to evoke the hoped-for gasps and guffaws. After the submergence of AWA into AWOC, not a single house meeting was held.

Father McCullough is modest to a fault. He believed in his own position, but did not believe he had the right to make its adoption the price of his continued participation in AWOC. He is also patient to a fault. Over and over again, when friends begged him to draw the strategic lines clearly and publicly, he said, "Give Smitty a chance. He's feeling his way. I think he'll come around to the local people if you give him a little more time."

The "little more time" grew from weeks to months to years. McCullough never joined the issue frontally. He continued to lend his support to AWOC by appearing at pitiful "mass meetings," invariably held in the vicinity of skid row and attended principally by down-and-outers looking for a warm place to spend the evening. When it came his turn to speak, he limited himself to a few homilies based on *Rerum novarum* or *Quadragessimo anno,* and always ended as cheerfully as he could: "Don't get discouraged. Keep going."

During 1958–59, McCullough had conclusively demonstrated that the winter months were ideal for organizing the Stockton area home guard. But in December, 1960, Norman Smith moved AWOC's entire resources 550 miles south, to El Centro. Loyal to the end, McCullough drove the 550 miles along with Father McDonnell. They appeared at strike meetings to deliver invocations, speak briefly to the workers, and, on at least one occasion, lead in the singing of union songs. They had often done as much within their own diocese; this time they miscalculated.

Imperial County was in the San Diego diocese. Charles Buddy, then bishop of the diocese, was quite different from Archbishop Mitty of San Francisco in his views toward the involvement of priests in agricultural organizing and other efforts at social justice. Buddy filed a protest with Mitty. The aging Mitty was then suffering his terminal illness, and archdiocesan business was being conducted by his chancellor. If Mitty had been physically able to handle Bishop Buddy's complaint, he probably would have defended his "problem children" as he had done before, and then called them in for a quiet talk. Lacking the status of bishop, however, the chancellor evidently felt he had to mollify Buddy.

After twelve years, the Mission Band was dismantled. McDonnell went to Mexico, to study at Ivan Illich's Center for Intercultural Documentation, prior to working among the poor of Brazil. McCullough was sent to a dying parish in downtown Oakland. He was ordered to avoid further public statements on agricultural labor and, in effect, to cut his ties with the movement. He had taken a solemn vow of obedience; he obeyed.

Emotionally exhausted, Father McCullough went into "retreat" for several weeks. Friends watched, expecting that when his energies revived he would throw himself into the civil rights movement and the organization of urban poverty neighborhoods. The Oakland parish was ideally suited to such work. But when McCullough returned from the wilderness, he did not re-enter the arena. He tried to get out: out of the archdiocese, out of the country, out of everything except the Church itself. He sought a transfer to Central or South America, but unlike Father McDonnell, he was unsuccessful.

A new generation—of civil rights workers, housewives, students, Protestant ministers, and others—has given the farm labor movement a broader base than ever before. Most of these people have never heard of the priest-organizer of the 1950's who brought to the movement unexampled energy, good sense, and good humor. He was God's laughing man, and proved that reverence and joy can form an unusually effective combination. No one has ever organized farm workers more successfully than Father Thomas A. McCullough during the months in which he was free to translate moral and practical convictions into action.

Once, in the spring of 1965, McCullough slipped into a rally for Cesar Chavez and the Delano grape strikers. A friend was indignant that every minor union official in the area was called upon to say a few words, but no one recognized the pioneer whose ideas had come to flower in the Delano movement. McCullough only chuckled. "The woods are full of us old gaffers [he was just forty-two; slightly older than Chavez himself] who have had something to do with organizing farm workers at one time or another. You know what we ought to do? After the thing is really over, and all the contracts have been signed, we old-timers ought to throw a reunion for ourselves. We can have a barbecue or something, and a couple of beers, and sit around and swap stories about the way it used to be. We'll invite Ernie Galarza. And old Smitty. And maybe we can even get Mc-Donnell up from Brazil . . ." He looked nostalgic for a moment. And then he laughed.

After his assignment in Oakland, and another in Brentwood, Father McCullough was given his own parish. He is now pastor of St. Ambrose Church in Berkeley, just a few blocks from where he grew up. His parishioners are workingmen and their families. In a sense, he has come home, after thirty years. But there are those who feel his home, in a more real sense, will always be in Stockton, among the wetbacks, braceros, Filipinos, and Mexican-Americans to whom he devoted himself and his vision in the heat haze of summer, the peat dust storms of spring, and the ground fogs of deep winter.

5. The Convert: Fred Van Dyke

Fred Van Dyke's face is tanned, warm, guileless, inviting of confidences, like the land itself. His face has had the dust from the land upon it a thousand times and more, as he drove the heavy equipment that levels, plows, harrows, plants, ridges, sprays, fertilizes, cultivates. His eyes have the look which comes only from working in the sun for many years. A good face, a smiling face, even an irresistible face. Everyone likes Fred Van Dyke. That is, everyone used to, before he "changed."

The road to Damascus for Fred Van Dyke was his race for Congress in 1958. A tyro in politics, he waged a highly unorthodox campaign: unorthodox for a largely agricultural district; especially unorthodox for a candidate who was himself a farmer, the son and grandson of farmers.

In his campaign, not only did he talk with his fellow growers, but with everyone else he could, including the Mexican-Americans and Filipinos in the shoestring communities and hidden fringe areas of the Fifteenth Congressional District. In this process, he was converted in his thinking about agricultural workers, and about his own role as an agricultural employer.

Grandfather Van Dyke came to California in the late 1800's and established a ranch in the hills of Mendocino County. His son, Claude, moved to San Joaquin County and went into farming near Linden. Fred's brother, Jim, became an attorney, but Fred says, "All I ever wanted to be was a farmer." He served a long apprenticeship. Claude Van Dyke did not pamper his sons.

"We learned what it is like to get out and bend our backs," Fred recalls. "The first job I ever had was picking hops. Did you ever pick hops? It's work!"

He was also learning other things that a real farmer needs to know: different types of soil and the crops for which they are best suited; irrigating; fertilizers; the maintenance of equipment; deciding what to plant, how much of it, and when; arranging to sell produce at the best price, to a cannery, a wholesaler, a winery, or taking a chance on the auction market; keeping cost accounts and payroll records. These he learned from his father, his neighbors and friends, from listening as men talked, and from personal experience. "I never got any good out of a book about farming," he says. "I don't believe I ever called on the county extension agent. I knew more than they could possibly know about my farm. There are no exact rules. Every farm is a little different."

He attended college in Stockton for two years, then spent a year at the University of California in Berkeley. Before he graduated, World War II began. He enlisted in the Navy as a Seaman, First Class, and was discharged four and a half years later as a Lieutenant, JG, his health damaged from a mine explosion in the Pacific. He married Carolyn Smythe, daughter of a ranching family in the Linden area. For a time he served as field man for the Holly Sugar Company, but by 1950 had recovered his health sufficiently to go into farming on his own. By borrowing money, he bought the two-thirds interest of his brothers-in-law, and the Smythe Ranch became the Van Dyke Ranch.

Fred Van Dyke had a vocation for farming, and he took pride in it. "Some people think that any numbskull can be a farmer," he says scornfully. "That's crazy! To be a good farmer is as hard as being a good college professor or anything else." He was contemptuous of what he called "phony farmers" who used the land for speculation or as a tax write-off. He told a Congressional committee in 1961:

> . . . it is time to cry halt to the phony farming . . . it is time to take farming out of the hands of the shippers, packers, canners, truckers, lawyers, doctors, baseball players, movie stars, and tired businessmen . . . it is time to return farming to real farmers, who know a nematode from a wire worm, and a hawk from a handsaw. . . .

The Van Dyke Ranch was devoted largely to row crops, the riskiest type of farming. If a man is a Midwestern corn-hog farmer, he raises corn and hogs year in and year out. If he is a Great Plains wheat farmer or a Mississippi Delta cotton farmer, there is never any question about what he will plant. If he has fruit or nut trees or grape vines, he cannot change varieties from year to year. A row-crop farmer, however, begins each season with nothing on his farm but the soil itself and an irrigation system. In most parts of California, the climate permits him a great variety of choices. He may grow any of twenty or twenty-five different crops equally successfully in terms of quantity and quality, but all would not be equally successful financially. There are no price supports for these crops. The grower must try to anticipate, six months in advance or more, what market conditions are likely to be at the time his crop is harvested.

Fred Van Dyke has described the process in his own way:

"It's like dogs sniffing around each other. You sniff around for any clues, any hot tips. Some of the guys must use tea leaves! Some fellows seem to have an intuition, and they do well consistently. Some are really pathetic. Whatever they guess, it always seems to turn out wrong. Most have run-of-the-mill luck. Sometimes they make it, sometimes they don't. Some system! In fact, there is no system. The thinking of the average tomato grower isn't much more rational than this: 'Well, old Charlie is putting in two hundred acres this year instead of a hundred and fifty. He did all right last year, so he must know something. I'll take a chance and put in fifty acres more myself.' It's really incredible! These are grown-up men, businessmen with investments of hundreds of thousands of dollars in what they are doing, and they haven't worked out anything better than a game of roulette!"

Van Dyke did his best to take the guesswork out of his row-crop farming. He did research on warehouse inventories from the previous year's canning operations; he read the *Wall Street Journal* and other financial periodicals. And he used his own logic. He knew that if a substantial number of tomato growers planted an extra fifty acres because "old Charlie" was doing so, the added production would tend to depress prices. If he had any one rule of thumb to guide his row-crop farming, it was to do what the others were not doing. In this sense, he was an innovator from the start of his farming career. He was also an innovator in certain technological experiments, such as a device for semimechanizing his cucumber harvest.

As long as Van Dyke was a maverick within the framework of the established values and assumptions, he was well liked and respected by his fellow growers. He played the game and he was good at it. He added to the Van Dyke Ranch until it reached nine hundred acres. He belonged to the Farm Bureau, the Tomato Growers Association, and other grower organizations and was an officer in some of them.

He was active in civic groups. Always a sports enthusiast, he was one of the prime organizers of the Stockton Relays, an annual track and field meet with internationally known athletes. He became an elder of the Presbyterian Church. His family grew until he had two daughters and four sons. Fred Van Dyke was a happy and successful man, his world a sunny world, and the sun was at its brightest in 1958.

Van Dyke, just turned forty, decided to run for Congress in 1958. It seemed a reasonable decision. For some time, he had been playing an increasingly active part in Republican politics, and the Republican Party had been firmly in control of the state government for almost eighty years. To be sure, Van Dyke's district, embracing San Joaquin and Stanislaus counties, had a Democratic incumbent, John McFall. The incumbent always has the advantage, but it appeared by no means an impossible advantage.

The story of Fred Van Dyke might have been very different if Senator William F. Knowland had not made a shambles of the California Republican Party that year. Knowland wanted to be governor of California, rather than minority leader of the U.S. Senate. To this end, he pressured Goodwin J. Knight to leave the governorship and run for the Senate. Confronted with familiar names running for unfamiliar offices, and perhaps disenchanted by Knowland's methods, hundreds of thousands of voters rebelled. Pat Brown was swept into the governorship along with most other Democratic candidates. In the rout, Fred Van Dyke was defeated by John McFall.

During his Congressional campaign, Fred Van Dyke's thinking about agricultural labor and economics began to change. Because he is the kind of a man he is, in time it would have changed anyway—but probably not as far and certainly not as fast. For three months, from August to November, he knocked on doors at least part of every day. He usually worked on his farm until late afternoon. After showering and changing clothes, and sometimes without even pausing for dinner, he drove to town for several hours of door-to-door canvassing.

Some of the people on whom he called were prosperous growers like himself, some were middle-class artisans and professionals. Other candidates would have stopped there. But Van Dyke moved on, into places like "Goat Valley," Boggs Tract, and the Mosswood area of Stockton, where he met the elderly poor, the disabled poor, and those who were poor because they were agricultural workers. Talking to these men and women in their own homes, Van Dyke confronted the farm labor problem in a way no San Joaquin Valley congressman, and perhaps no candidate for any other office, ever has.

Explaining the impact of the confrontation upon him, Van Dyke wrote later:

> I had been rubbing shoulders with farm workers most of my life, one way or another. For the previous eight years I had been hiring them. But I hadn't been in farm workers' homes before, and this was the first time I had ever seen how they and their families live. In the midst of the richest farming area in the world, I found most of them living in shacks. . . . I found that I couldn't shrug off their poverty as something that was their own fault. They were good people. They weren't loafers, they weren't alcoholics, they weren't stupid or dumb. They were serious, responsible people, trying to make a living in the trade where they had their skills, for farm work is skilled work.

Van Dyke was brave enough to face the logical but painful conclusion. As he put it in a public speech: "I've hired these people. I've been their source of income. Therefore, I am responsible for this poverty and privation."

The more he thought about the problem, the more he became convinced that the most pernicious single feature of the agricultural system was the bracero program. He had used bracero labor himself, had subscribed to the myth that "Americans just won't do farm work." Now, in his door-to-door calls, he met hundreds of San Joaquin County residents who at one time had picked tomatoes, the largest of all the bracero-using crops. Clearly, it was not farm work, as such, that "Americans just won't do." Something had changed. Equally clearly, the change was in wages. Eighteen to twenty-five cents a box had been the rate in 1950, with most of the picking done by domestic workers. Eight years later, eleven cents a box was the prevailing rate, with virtually all the picking done by braceros.

Doctrinaire liberal critics of braceroism had a myth of their own: that bracero users were unvarnished brigands, waxing rich from peon labor, easily able to pay a living wage if they chose to do so. Van Dyke knew that in most cases this was untrue. He was beginning to see that the system was hurting growers and workers alike. And he was beginning to perceive how feeble were farmers' attempts to bargain with the buyers of their products. Year after year, about a month before the harvest was to begin, the tomato growers of San Joaquin County met to talk about prices. Year after year, they resolved that, this time, they would stand firm on a fair price, usually much higher than the canneries were offering.

Their resolve never seemed to hold. Cannery agents visited them, one by one, painting vivid word-pictures of the enormous holdover from the previous year's pack, and whispering that some growers had already signed at the canneries' figure. Torn, the grower would remember the agreement to "hold the line this year," and then gaze at his green tomatoes in the field, already beginning to show a little pink here and there. In a day or two, after a little dickering, he would accept the agent's final offer, slightly above the original, but below what the growers had agreed was "rock-bottom." And once a few growers had signed, the stampede was on.

Tomato growers tried to survive the smaller profit per unit by increasing production. They leased more land, planted more tomatoes, and knew that harvest labor would be no problem since the government would import all the braceros they wanted. So the spiral went, year after year: more tomatoes, more braceros, lower prices, lower wages, more tomatoes, more braceros, lower prices, lower wages. . . .

As Van Dyke put it, the tomato growers in his area were "hooked on a peon labor jag." By having all the braceros they asked for, delivered to them at virtually any wage they cared to pay, they thought they could "beat the system"—could somehow get away with ignoring the demand of consumers for what they grew, and the backlog of supplies in the warehouses. Van Dyke now realized that he and his fellow growers were wrong; they could no more repeal the law of supply and demand than they could repeal the law of gravity.

At the start of his campaign, Van Dyke announced that he regarded the bracero program as "necessary": a stand identical to that of Congressman McFall. Although his view changed during the course of the campaign, he felt that if he publicly announced the change, it would appear to be only a calculated appeal for liberal votes. It was not until December, 1958, that Fred Van Dyke openly acknowledged that he had been mistaken on the bracero question.

Van Dyke's first step as a convert was to become active in Father

Thomas McCullough's Agricultural Workers Association. He spoke at its meetings and helped in every way he could. His critics whispered that he already had his eye on the 1960 elections and was making a play for the farm labor vote. Quite aside from the fact that this would have been completely uncharacteristic of the man, there was, and still is, no such thing as a "farm labor vote" in San Joaquin County or anywhere else.

When the AWA went out of existence in favor of the AFL-CIO's Agricultural Workers Organizing Committee, Van Dyke may have swallowed once or twice. Big Labor is quite a different thing from a small, local, independent association led by a priest. Nevertheless, he cast his lot boldly with the new organization.

At five o'clock on the afternoon of July 2, 1959, still wearing dusty denims and boots from a day's work driving his D2 tractor, Fred Van Dyke walked into AWOC headquarters at 805 East Weber Street in Stockton. He was carrying a handwritten manuscript which, in its way, was equivalent to Paul's first epistle to the Romans. Van Dyke's epistle, entitled "An Open Letter to My Fellow Farmers," was reproduced by the thousands. Van Dyke himself paid the postage in a mailing to every grower in San Joaquin County. Highlights of this letter:

As a farmer, I will support the unionization of agricultural labor.

It has been said that a strike at harvest would ruin the farmer. . . . The farmer who cooperates with the agricultural workers' union has at least as much to gain from the union as the union has to gain from him. Contracts signed in advance of the season could well contain no-strike clauses . . . the farmer would enjoy greater labor stability than he does today.

It has been said that agriculture . . . cannot afford to increase wages. I firmly believe that unionization of farm labor will prod farmers into organizing on their own behalf in order to receive higher prices for their products. . . .

The large farm syndicates which are able to hire labor at very low wages will be the only group with a difficult period of adjustment . . . the family farm will benefit most . . . the small farmer . . . attempts to do as much of his own work as possible. He is then automatically competing for a wage in the farm labor market . . . he is unable to support his family on the equivalent of the wages the syndicate pays. He is forced to sell out to the syndicate. . . .

. . . I realize that some of my friends and colleagues will disagree with my conclusions. . . . However, having spent a lifetime associating with farmers, I believe I can say most of them are fair-minded, reasonable men. . . .

I feel it is my duty, as a farmer, and a man of God, to attempt to instil my influence into this new union so that it may better become a strong force for the good of the workers, employers, and all society. . . . I feel it is my duty also, to make my stand public, through this open letter, in order that some, at least, may learn from my observations and accept, rather than fight, a movement they will never halt.

The tone and most of the themes which Van Dyke was to elaborate in later speeches, writings, and testimony were contained in this open letter: his use of hard-headed economic arguments combined with moral fervor; his passionate belief in the free enterprise system; his equally passionate belief in independent farming as opposed to the "syndicate"; his optimism bordering on naïveté.

Before long, Van Dyke had the opportunity to test in practice some of his theoretical propositions. He had just bought a ninety-acre vineyard near Lodi, and began the 1959 harvest with a crew of local grape cutters, employing them under the usual piece-rate system. These grapes were for table use and subject to inspection for sugar content and freedom from mold. He offered the cutters ten cents per box more than the going rate, with the understanding they would pack a high quality product. Despite this, the grapes failed to pass inspection. "I don't blame the cutters too much," he said later. "I do blame the piece-rate system." By its very nature, that system prods the worker toward greater quantity rather than quality.

Van Dyke recounted his experience to an AWOC representative, who offered to provide him with the necessary number of cutters for the duration of the season, and to designate a field steward to represent them. Hourly wages, rather than a piece rate, were agreed upon, in writing. Van Dyke later described the results in an article.

The union crew worked every day I needed it, between September 25 and October 16. On days when I needed fifteen workers, the hiring hall sent me fifteen; on days I needed thirty workers, the hiring hall sent me thirty. I got all my grapes in without the worries I would have had otherwise. I was freed to spend my time locating boxes and gondolas, hauling grapes, and dealing with buyers. Not a single box of grapes harvested by my union crew was rejected at an inspection station. The minor problems which arose inevitably in the course of the season were resolved in discussions between myself or my representative and the field steward representing the workers.

It has been said for many years . . . that a hiring hall system will not work in agriculture. I know from personal experience that it *will*.

Van Dyke's early predictions regarding the "fair-mindedness" and "reasonableness" of his fellow growers proved overly optimistic. Not even his lifelong personal friends were able to follow his arguments. On the other hand, these arguments—their force enhanced by the fact that they came from someone who had "met a payroll"—were like rain on the desert for church and liberal groups, whose spokesmen had been discredited for years on the grounds that they were "outsiders" who "just didn't understand agriculture."

Van Dyke quickly became something of a celebrity within the farm labor movement. He was invited to join a National Advisory Committee on Farm Labor which included Helen Gahagan Douglas, Archbishop Robert Lucey, Herbert Lehman, Frank Graham, A. Philip Randolph, and Eleanor Roosevelt. It amused Van Dyke that on the committee's letterhead, he, a staunch defender of capitalism, was juxtaposed with the elder statesman of socialism, Norman Thomas.

Van Dyke was invited to speak in Chicago at a National Conference to Stabilize Migrant Labor, on November 21, 1959. With assistance from the AWOC research department, he prepared an unusually comprehensive statement, which was subsequently published. Under the title, "Responsibilities of the Agricultural Employer for the Stabilization of Migrant Labor," he wrote about legal, economic, and moral responsibilities.

Of legal responsibilities, he said:

One of the premises on which our society operates is the premise that . . . when a person enjoys the privilege of employing the labor of other persons, he automatically takes on a number of legal responsibilities . . . in what we usually call "social legislation". . . . The extension of such legislation [to agriculture] would not only protect farm workers, but would protect responsible farm employers themselves against the unfair competition of . . . growers who exploit and abuse their employees.

It was typical of Van Dyke that he was able to find many reasons why growers should change their practices, not from abstractions such as social justice, but from sheer self-interest. Most of the speech was devoted to what he called "economic responsibilities," and represented Van Dyke at his most practical. The essence of his argument was that growers are a kind of businessmen; that the most basic of all their responsibilities is to be good businessmen; and that it is self-defeating to try to rest any business on an underpaid, insecure, demoralized labor force.

He pointed out that under existing farm labor conditions, California's agricultural workers often cannot afford to buy the very goods they produce. Using Department of Agriculture statistics, he demonstrated that farm labor families spend 35 percent less than other families for food, and that their diets lean toward cheap, starchy, filling items, rather than fruits, vegetables, meat and dairy products. In this way, California growers are writing off from 5 to 10 percent of their potential market, and, Van Dyke noted, that is usually the margin between success and failure in farming or any other business. Warming to the theme of unsound business practices in agriculture, he declared:

It is almost incredible to me that my neighbor should plant fifty acres of new peaches while the man across the road is pulling his trees because he can't make a living on the price he receives for peaches. That happened this year. It cannot be permitted to continue to happen. Planning is going to have to govern the planting within each area.

He hastened to add that he hoped the planning would be done by growers themselves, rather than by bureaucrats in Sacramento or in Washington, D.C. He then spoke of the equally pressing need for planning the efficient use of labor.

The most important resource in agriculture—more important than soil, more important than water, more important than seed—is human beings. . . . I have seen, as recently as the past few months, able-bodied and experienced farm workers who wanted to work, idle in the very midst of so-called "labor shortages." The reason is that growers tend to view their crews as their personal property, and if a crew is finished at 10 A.M., it must lay off until the grower calls for its services again. . . . This sort of labor waste is going to have to be replaced by cooperation and coordination.

Van Dyke scorned the canard that normal labor laws are inapplicable to agriculture because farm workers are "unemployables."

"If we don't hire these people, who will?" [some growers say]. What they really mean is that physical, mental, emotional, and social cripples are willing to work for . . . low wages. . . . I say that it is not a favor to anyone concerned for agriculture to serve as a social welfare agency. If some farm workers are in fact "unemployable," let the regular social agencies care for them. A healthy industry cannot be built on substandardness.

In discussing "moral responsibilities," he expressed doubt that material changes alone would be sufficient to overcome the demoralization of the farm labor market:

I think it very important that growers offer work which is acceptable not only in its tangible aspects, but in its more subtle aspects as well. We must have an end to the totally false assumption that farm labor is dishonorable and degrading.

Van Dyke suggested that growers had contributed to this false assumption by their use of braceros and their cultivation of the myth that farm work is "Mexican work." He implied that growers might overcome the myth by going into the fields and helping with the work themselves, and he suggested that it was not growers alone who had the responsibility to make agriculture a prideful part of the American economic family.

If the harvest is as important to the community as we are told it is, the community itself should pitch in to relieve whatever "labor shortages" may arise.

At the conclusion of this speech, he received a standing ovation. He later said, "It was the greatest moment of my life—next to my wedding day and the birth of our first child."

On behalf of the National Advisory Committee on Farm Labor, Van Dyke flew to Washington, D.C., in March, 1960, to testify before the House Committee on Agriculture, against the bracero program. The following month, again representing the National Advisory Committee, he testified before a subcommittee which was drafting an agricultural plank for the 1960 Democratic national platform. Afterward he said, "There were these big-name economists sitting there with open mouths. They just couldn't understand what I was saying about supply and demand. Somebody is nuts—either them or me!" The platform on which John F. Kennedy ran that fall did not contain Van Dyke's recommendation of explicit opposition to Public Law 78.

His "fellow farmers," as Fred Van Dyke liked to call them, tolerated his idiosyncratic opinions as long as the farm labor wars were waged only with words and ideas. When the battle was really joined, however, he learned how the flower of friendship can wither in the furnace of economic interest. In May, 1960, AWOC conducted its first major strike, against "the world's largest cherry grower," Fred Podesta, whose ranch was close to Van Dyke's. The strike was effective; Podesta was adamant; some cherries were lost. Feelings grew bitter and sharply divided. One was either for or against the union; either for or against the growers. Van Dyke, who had tried to move in both circles and to serve the industry of agriculture as a whole, found he could not do so.

Men he had known since boyhood no longer spoke to him when they met on the street. He and his wife did not receive the invitations they formerly would have received as a matter of course. Fred tried to joke about it, but the jokes grew forced. His children were attending public schools in Linden, a growers' community. They began to hear uncomplimentary things about their father. As they rode their bicycles home from school, pick-up trucks whizzed by, dangerously close. A coincidence? Perhaps. But Fred Van Dyke began to drive his children to and from school.

His wife received anonymous telephone calls at night when Fred was attending farm labor meetings. "What's the matter with that husband of yours?" a voice would ask; or "You'd better start showing some sense"; or heavy breathing and nothing more.

By this time, as one of his forms of protest against prevailing practices in the farm labor market, Van Dyke was growing only crops which could be harvested without hand labor—sugar beets, field corn, and grain—even though this represented a significant reduction in income for him. In September, 1960, a barley field adjoining his home was burned. He had to stand on his roof with a garden hose to prevent the house from burning. Although it seemed a clear case of arson by someone aggrieved by Van Dyke's opinions, nothing was ever proved.

On that bleak, blazing September day Fred Van Dyke asked himself whether he had a moral right to endanger his wife and children through activities which were not of their own choosing. If only he, himself, had been involved, he would have challenged his new-found, anonymous enemies to come into the open and fight. But he had responsibilities which preceded those he had assumed in farming and in the farm labor movement. He wrestled with his dilemma in silent agony, feeling that the decision was the sort a man must make for himself, by himself. The easy thing would have been to bow out of the farm labor movement and return to the joyful life revolving around the twin poles of his farm and his family. But the polar equilibrium of his world had been altered for all time by his commitment to the farm labor movement. He had to choose between the two poles; he could not have both.

In the darkest hour of his life, Fred Van Dyke knew that he had to sacrifice his love for farming rather than his love for his wife and children. Less than a year before, he had concluded a speech with the trusting prediction, "By the time my boys are old enough to take over my ranch from me . . . within the next brief arc of history, I believe, will grow a great [agricultural] industry—and from it, great leaders for our America, and for our world." Now there would be no ranch for his boys to take over. Van Dyke decided to sell his 900 acres. Toward the end of 1960, he moved his family to a beach community in southern California where their home was accessible only by passing the scrutiny of a watchman on duty twenty-four hours a day.

He continued to speak on farm labor matters, but by now he had concluded, as Father McCullough had earlier concluded, that most of his "fellow farmers" were not going to be moved by moral appeals or economic reasoning: they would not update their industry until until they had to in order to survive, and the only source of that kind of pressure was the farm labor movement.

A speech entitled "Economics and Conscience," which he delivered in October, 1960, to a church group in Stockton contained more moral fervor, and has been more widely quoted, than any of his other statements.

> I do not care what argument the Associated Farmers and Farm Bureau may advance. They complain about a cost-price squeeze. They claim that agriculture is "unique" because it deals with perishable commodities. They complain about the unpredictability of the weather. All this is so much sophistry, rationalization, and evasion. All of it is irrelevant when compared to even one single child weeping from hunger. . . . The moral argument, the humanitarian argument, closes debate without any further evidence required. The argument based upon conscience demands—and I say *demands*—that existing arrangements in agricultural labor be rethought and rebuilt from the very ground up. The question of how this is to be done is secondary. The first step is to recognize that it *must* be done. Then ways will be found. . . .
>
> I would like to believe that the industry of agriculture might be saved from its foolishness on the strength of logic. . . . But I have been forced regretfully to the conclusion that too many of my fellow farmers . . . have become habituated over the years to "going it alone," and they will apparently not give up this habit on the basis of friendly persuasion by me or anyone else. . . . There is only one force in our society of countervailing forces which can bring about this change: the force of organized labor.
>
> You may say to me, "That will mean giving up freedom and independence." I say to you that the only freedom the average farmer has today is the freedom to go broke. And I say to you that bankruptcy is the shortest road to slavery. The day that men representing me and my fellow farmers sit down across the table from men representing the laborers who work for us, will in fact be an Independence Day for farmers . . . we will be free from our own excesses under a system . . . which has been marked, not by freedom, but by license.

On March 7, 1961, Fred Van Dyke delivered one of his last public statements on farm labor at a hearing by the House Committee on Agriculture on the question of extending Public Law 78. With the exception of an AWOC representative who was present, no one there realized that Van Dyke was saying once more the things which had been his undoing.

Everything I do or say on Public Law 78 or any other issue in this field has but one purpose: to enable the farmer and the farm workers—both of them together—to survive in dignity in a free society. There *is* dignity, gentlemen, in agriculture. For the moment it has shrunk under the onslaught of misguided legislation such as Public Law 78. But given the chance, it can survive and it can flower. The dignity inherent in agriculture deserves to survive, no less than our free society itself deserves to survive.

Van Dyke's appeals to economic and moral principles were ignored, as he knew they would be. It began to snow as he returned to his hotel with the AWOC representative. For an instant, the scene seemed surrealistic. He said, "Why am I not where I belong, in San Joaquin County? It's time to put in tomatoes. What am I doing here?" Then the scene came back into focus, and he walked on in the snow.

Fred Van Dyke no longer makes public statements, although he is still listed on the letterhead of the National Advisory Committee on Farm Labor. He is back in Stockton, but he is now a stockbroker. He owns a few acres of walnuts, but he no longer works closely with the growing things he loves.

Not long ago, a friend—one of the few who know the full story of what Fred Van Dyke lost through his conversion to the farm labor movement—asked him, "Do you ever think you may have made a mistake, Fred, in getting involved as you did?"

"I was ahead of my time," he answered. "I stuck my neck way out. If you think those things are mistakes, then, sure, I made a mistake. But it was something that had to be done some day. If it hadn't been me, it would have been somebody else, five years from now, or ten years from now. Somebody has to go out on limbs. Otherwise, nothing would ever change, and we would all still live in caves."

"Would you do anything differently, if you had it to do over again?"

Van Dyke thought for only a moment before saying firmly, "No, I would not."

All authentic social movements occasionally make converts from the ranks of what might seem to be its natural enemies. Fred Van Dyke was not the first grower to support the farm labor movement. For instance, Bertha Rankin, a landowner in Weedpatch, near Arvin, donated land and a building for the National Farm Labor Union to use as its headquarters in the 1947–50 strike against Di Giorgio. And Fred Van Dyke will not be the last grower converted. Particularly as the movement draws nearer to its goal, there will be others.

One of the most distinguishing and endearing characteristics of the convert is his trust. Van Dyke had faith that his fellow growers would see the light as he had seen it; that reason, logic, and demonstrable economic evidence would prevail; that his friends would remain his friends; that his transparent decency would protect him.

This quality makes converts especially vulnerable. Persons with longer experience in a movement know that justice, personal decency, logic, and facts do not always triumph. Converts learn these lessons the hard way. They find that their former associates view them as apostates, and their new-found associates may question their sincerity, too. They sometimes lose more than anyone else in the course of a movement—their friends, their livelihood, and their trust.

But all is not invariably loss for the convert. He stands to gain the respect of those who understand—and of himself.

6. Man of Fire: Ernesto Galarza

Among the extraordinary persons who have made the farm workers' cause their own, one of the most exceptional is Ernesto Galarza, a wiry man with a shock of graying hair and penetrating eyes under full black eyebrows, a brilliant speaker and writer, a doctor of philosophy from Columbia University.

Galarza fought, at times simultaneously and almost single-handedly, the power of agribusiness, federal and state governments, and Big Labor. In the uneven contest, he may seem to have lost, as the world usually reckons winning and losing. But social movements have their own secret reckonings. Galarza kept alive the embers of the farm labor movement in California during a long night in which they came close to being extinguished altogether.

Ernesto Galarza was born in Tepic, Nayarit, on Mexico's Pacific Coast, at about the time the Mexican revolution was being conceived in secret meetings led by Francisco Madero and others. In 1910, the revolution reached the shooting stage; Galarza's parents fled the country. One of his earliest memories is of crouching on the floor of a train bearing them north to the border as bullets spattered on the outside.

The Galarzas settled in Sacramento, where Ernesto had the opportunity, denied many a Mexican child before and since, of attending school regularly. In the summers, he did farm labor of various types.

A group of his high school teachers insisted that he go on to college. The leader of this group was an alumnus of Occidental, a small liberal arts college in southern California, and Galarza was turned in that direction. He obtained an academic scholarship, and in 1923 entered Occidental College. Since his scholarship did not meet room, board, and incidental expenses, he waited on tables, mowed lawns, and did whatever other work he could find. Periodically, he drove to Sacramento in his Model A Ford to help with problems of his brothers and sisters; as the eldest, he had become head of the family upon the death of his parents.

He went to graduate school at Stanford University, where he majored in economics, but then and throughout his life, he creatively combined an interest in the humanities and the social sciences. When he writes on economics, "the Dismal Science," it is with a grace, wit, and style which are rare in any field.

During his year at Stanford, Galarza met and married Mae Taylor. After he received his master's degree, they left for Columbia University, where he had won a fellowship to pursue his doctorate. He was almost certainly influenced by the School of Education at Columbia University, although he did not study directly under John Dewey. His entire adult life has been marked by a special concern for education. It was no accident that when the time came to choose a title for himself in the farm labor movement, it was Director of Research and Education.

By 1934, Galarza had satisfied all the requirements for his doctor of philosophy degree except the dissertation. He needed full-time employment; by now, he and Mae had two daughters. For something over a year, he was employed by the Foreign Policy Association as a specialist in Latin affairs. Then, in 1936, he was offered a job with the Pan American Union as a research associate in education. He accepted gladly, since the position seemed an ideal outlet for several of his skills and interests, including his belief in education as an instrument of social change. Through his association with the Pan American Union, he hoped to help bring justice to the Spanish and Portuguese Americas without the kind of violent revolution he had witnessed in his childhood in Mexico.

During his years with the Pan American Union, Galarza worked on his dissertation, a study of the electric light and power industry in Mexico. It was completed in 1943, and Galarza received his doctorate from Columbia in 1944.

On Galarza's recommendation, a Division of Labor and Social Information was created within the Pan American Union in 1940, and he was made its first director. The job gave him a modest voice in policy recommendations, allowed him to travel rather extensively throughout the hemisphere, and supported his family in comfort. Later he said, "I would be there yet if I had been willing to turn to stone like the building we were housed in, and the diplomats who came there to keep us from accomplishing anything. Animated marble busts!"

In 1942, the World War II version of the bracero program was enacted. As a labor agreement between two member nations of the Pan American Union, it fell within Galarza's portfolio. He obtained permission to conduct an investigation of the program from the standpoint of its effect upon relations between the "good neighbors," Mexico and the United States.

Galarza bypassed the snares of bureaucracy and conducted the investigation in his own way. He went directly into the camps where braceros were housed and talked with them about their concerns: wages, food, medical care, recreation, their families, whatever. On the basis of visits to twenty camps, detailed interviews with two hundred of the workers, and brief discussions with hundreds more, he wrote a "Personal and Confidential Memorandum on Mexican Contract Workers in the United States." In effect, he concluded that the contract labor program, far from being administered as an instrument of neighborliness, was being used as an instrument through which the larger neighbor exploited the smaller.

Galarza stayed nearly eleven years with the Pan American Union. The break came in 1946, precipitated by an event which he summarized before a Senate committee six years later, in a characteristic mixture of anger, eloquence, high principle, and humor:

I resigned voluntarily . . . on account of illness. I suffered a stroke of nausea when I observed at close quarters the betrayal of Bolivian miners and farm workers by the United States Department of State. This betrayal led to the installation in Bolivia of a coalition government composed of four parts tin barons, three parts corporation farmers, and two parts Communist Party. Sinister in its origin, hypocritical in its execution, and tragic in its ending, this obscure but significant diplomatic incident has yet to receive the attention it deserves.

For a time Galarza was "at liberty." He could have had any of a number of academic or bureaucratic positions, some of them paying handsomely, but he was looking for something which would permit him to come directly to grips with social injustice, and he was willing to wait for the right opportunity.

For some years, Galarza had known of H. L. Mitchell and the

Southern Tenant Farmers Union, which, in 1945, had become the AFL's National Farm Labor Union. In 1947, Mitchell received a grant which made it possible for the NFLU to move outside its base in the South into California. It soon became apparent that the drive in California needed a Spanish-speaking organizer; a coming-together of the man and the job took place. In 1948, Galarza and his family moved to California, where the long NFLU strike against the Di Giorgio Fruit Company was already in progress.

The Galarza family home was established in San Jose, but Ernesto spent most of his time in the field, familiarizing himself with the changes in California agriculture since he had last done farm labor in the early 1920's. He was the very model of diplomacy, staying in the background while the Di Giorgio strike director, Hank Hasiwar, continued the activities which were already in motion. When Galarza eventually became his own strike director, Hasiwar returned his consideration with a loyalty rare in organized labor.

By 1950, Galarza felt ready for a major move. He was the principal organizer of an NFLU local in the area of Tracy, San Joaquin County, where most of the canning tomatoes in California were grown. The membership and staff decided to call a strike in September, 1950, to protest a wage cut in tomato picking.

Perhaps as many as three thousand workers became involved. Other unions and community groups did not respond as generously as they had three years earlier in the Di Giorgio strike, but one man did: Father Thomas McCullough. Years later he recalled, "We all fell in love with Ernie. The rest of us had been kind of fumbling around with the problem, and here was a man who really knew what he was doing! Boy, we thought, this is it! He was so dynamic. Such a grasp of the field. And how he can capture an audience! We thought, here's the leader we've all been waiting for!"

Large numbers of wetbacks were employed by the tomato growers at that time, but Galarza felt he could deal with the problem. "Despite all their handicaps, wetbacks are freer than braceros," he said. "They can walk off their jobs. Braceros can't." Some observers felt that the refusal of Teamster truck drivers to respect the NFLU picket lines was the most crucial factor in breaking the strike, but Galarza did not agree. "It wouldn't have made any difference if they drove through our lines, if there had been nobody behind the lines picking the tomatoes. What broke us was two thousand braceros, sent in to pick under Highway Patrol and police escort."

By the spring of 1951, Galarza was ready to try again. In many ways, the Imperial Valley was the most improbable of places for a fledgling union to try to organize agricultural workers. It was just across the border from a practically inexhaustible supply of cheap labor, and it was the bastion of an especially lawless brand of union-busting. Even today, there are those in health, welfare, law, and other fields who shrug their shoulders and say, "Imperial County? It's not part of the United States. It's another country."

At the same time, there were good reasons for going into the Imperial Valley. For nearly a quarter-century an undercurrent of Mexican self-organization had existed there, and Galarza was now confident of his ability to galvanize the latent militancy of Spanish-speaking workers. An even more important reason for the move was later expressed by Galarza in this way:

"Theoretically, it may have seemed that we should have stayed in Tracy, but we weren't able to operate on the basis of neat logic. We had to be fluid; we had to move wherever the wetback or bracero tides were running the highest. If we hadn't shifted here and there, plugging this weak spot in the dike, and then that, there wouldn't have been any dry land left anywhere in the state. By 1951, it was obvious that the major port of entry for the tide of Mexican nationals, legal and illegal, was Imperial County. The most useful thing we could do for the workers of the Tracy area, and every other part of the state, was to try to plug that hole."

The NFLU struck the Imperial Valley cantaloupe harvest in April, 1951. The immediate grievance was that the work, which had been done for years at piece rates, enabling skilled local crews to make fairly good earnings, had been shifted to a straight seventy cents an hour. Since Mexican nationals could survive on this, while American citizens could not, local workers were rapidly being forced out of the area.

When the U.S. Border Patrol proved lax in rounding up wetbacks, the union members made citizens' arrests of illegal entrants, and guarded the border to prevent their re-entry. Once again, however, the union underestimated the potentialities of the bracero system. On a number of ranches, braceros took the places of the wetbacks the union had removed; sometimes wetbacks were simply legalized on the spot by federal agents.

In the sense that the strike did not gain wage increases or contracts, it failed, but as Galarza explained:

"Many of our strikes had objectives other than the usual ones. If we talked in the usual terms, that was because the labor fakers back East didn't understand any other kind. In fact, the strike was quite successful in its underlying purpose, which was to get rid of the wetback traffic. The stink we raised played an important part in getting the Texas labor movement to pay attention to the problem, in getting a number of exposés published in national magazines, in getting some Congressional hearings, and in getting the entire Immigration and Naturalization Service reorganized in 1954."

In the summer of 1951, Congress enacted Public Law 78, placing the bracero system on a more permanent basis than before. The NFLU fought the law from its introduction at a Department of Labor conference in February, 1951, to its passage in July. Once the law was on the books, however, union strategists felt that until it came up for Congressional reconsideration in 1953, the best that could be done was to try to find ways to turn it to their advantage.

Galarza noted an obscure clause in the treaty with Mexico which implemented Public Law 78: "No Mexican workers shall be assigned to fill any job which is vacant because of a strike or lockout." He had confidence in a society of laws, and this treaty was part of the supreme law of the land.

With this confidence, Galarza returned to the Imperial Valley in May, 1952. He found the local farm labor force already almost decimated by the effects of Public Law 78. From nearly five thousand the year before, the number of local cantaloupe pickers had shrunk to fewer than a thousand. He did his best to rally those who remained, and proceeded with his test of the treaty between the United States and Mexico.

More than half of the local workers walked off the job. Under ordinary circumstances, this would have been economically effective. Public Law 78 was no ordinary circumstance, however. It was a simple matter for members of the growers' association who had more braceros than they could use—a common condition throughout the life of the system—to transfer their excess workers to fellow members who were being struck. Galarza complained to the authorities that this was a violation of the law. They promised to "investigate," but that was the last he heard of the matter. In June, the cantaloupe harvest was over; so were Galarza's illusions about government agencies, including those which were theoretically "labor-oriented."

During much of 1953 and 1954, Ernesto Galarza was in Louisiana helping to organize sugar-cane workers and small strawberry tenant farmers, whose earnings were often even lower than those of agricultural workers in California.

The 1953 effort was defeated by court injunctions. California growers have often obtained, from judges who are sometimes growers themselves, injunctions which limit the number and location of pickets. In Louisiana, however, injunctions prohibiting *all* picketing were obtained by corporate agricultural interests from their friends on the bench. The union's painstaking work of organizing two thousand people, and inducing them to leave their jobs, was nullified overnight.

Although the injunctions could not be set aside in time to save the union's 1953 efforts, the union appealed, hoping to keep the legal precedent from being used against it at other times and in other places. The Louisiana Supreme Court upheld the injunctions with these memorable words: "The guarantee of freedom of speech, even if picketing and speech are held to be identical, cannot be maintained in the face of such irreparable injury to property." Lacking the resources to appeal the decision to the United States Supreme Court in the usual manner, the union filed a pauper's oath, and a volunteer attorney, Daniel Pollitt, handled the case. Two years later, the Supreme Court set aside the injunctions on First Amendment grounds, but the damage to the union could not be undone.

Subsequent organizing efforts in Louisiana were destroyed in an even more remarkable manner. The rural-dominated state legislature enacted a "right to work" law in 1954. It was evidently a reprisal against the Louisiana labor movement for having supported the 1953 agricultural strike. The newly merged state AFL-CIO organization launched a campaign to repeal the "right-to-work" act, with strong support from the now renamed National Agricultural Workers Union. A repeal bill was introduced in the spring of 1956.

Without the knowledge of the NAWU, an agreement was worked out between the state labor federation and representatives of the American Sugar Cane League: the League would use its powerful influence to repeal the 1954 act—and substitute one applying only to agriculture.

In the legislative process, grower lobbyists and their beholden legislators amended the definition of "agricultural labor" to include cotton ginning and compressing, rice milling, sugar refining, and other work not included in the original agreement. Despite even this, the state AFL-CIO called the amended law "good legislation."

As Galarza pointed out, this put Louisiana in a distinguished position. Many states had many kinds of discriminatory legislation against farm workers, but Louisiana alone had a "right to work" law applying exclusively to agriculture. Furthermore, Galarza wrote, it "is the only so-called 'right to work' law on the books of any state in the Union which carries the endorsement of organized labor, AFL-CIO."

Galarza and H. L. Mitchell sought to have the national AFL-CIO repudiate Louisiana labor's position. They journeyed to a resort in the Pocono Mountains of Pennsylvania, where the AFL-CIO executive council was meeting in the fall of 1956. From the standpoint of the embattled little farm workers' union, the resort, owned by the International Ladies Garment Workers Union, was ironically named: Unity House. The NAWU's appeal was rejected.

The president and executive council of the AFL-CIO appeared wedded to a philosophy of labor Darwinism, under which the rule, survival of the fittest, applies to the evolution of trade unions as well as organic species. Given this philosophy, the position of the Louisiana AFL-CIO seemed perfectly reasonable: It is our job to look out for the interests of workers who are already organized and paying their dues; it is not our job to look out for anyone else; if the weak lose out, it is too bad, but it is their own fault for being weak.

To speak of turning points in men or movements is always something of a falsification. Such moments are always preceded by an accretion of experiences which point toward the eventual change. If the scales had not fallen from Galarza's eyes at Unity House, they would have fallen before long somewhere else, just as his final disillusionment with the U.S. Department of Labor would have taken place sooner or later if it had not occurred in the Imperial Valley in 1952.

Galarza left the Pocono Mountains with a burden under which a lesser man would have buckled. He was convinced now that in the task of organizing agricultural workers, he and his relative handful of co-workers were confronted with no fewer than three major classes of obstacles: first and most obvious, agricultural employers; second, the U.S. Department of Labor and state public employment services, with their control of the bracero program giving them a kind of power in labor-management relations never before or since wielded by government in this country; and third, organized labor itself.

The last of these obstacles was the most galling. It was not that labor, by and large, was hostile to the organization of agricultural workers. Scores of resolutions containing eloquent words about the "plight of the farm worker" were passed at conventions representing millions of organized workers. This rhetoric, however, only irritated Galarza, because it was so much less than he felt he had a right to expect from avowed friends. "We don't want their fine words," he said in a 1957 interview. "We want their support: financial, political, moral. When we go before a Congressional committee, for instance, we want to know that we're not being traded away in the back cloak-room. . . . We do not have that kind of assurance now."

Galarza undertook, simultaneously, to destroy the alliance between growers and government bureaucrats, and to shake organized labor out of its complacency. All the while, insofar as he was able, he maintained contact with farm workers in the Imperial Valley and other areas where the union had established footholds. He had neither large numbers of supporters, nor finances, nor friends in high places. His weapons were highly personal: the shield of research and analytical thought, the sword of the written and spoken word. Armed with these, he set forth to do battle with the fortified feudal cities of the bracero system, and the indifference of organized labor.

His basic tactic was to document the flouting of laws—the abuses, the corruption, the debasement, the scandals inherent in the bracero system—and to publicize his findings as widely as possible. If the growers and the government fought back, so much the better. Keep the controversy going, keep the pot boiling, keep the issue in the public eye: that was the most that could be hoped for in the short run. As long as the issue was open, there was always the possibility that some scandal would prove so odious, some salvo so explosive, that public indignation would be aroused and the somnolent democratic conscience stirred into action.

To be truly effective, the technique of *j'accuse* requires that the accuser have enough "troops" that the accused must pay attention. But Galarza was caught in a cruel moral dilemma. He could have gone to any number of places throughout the state and induced the local farm workers to protest visibly against the bracero system. This would have strengthened his hand in the mass media, in the halls of Congress, and in labor circles. It would also have left those workers defenseless. Under the bracero system, there was no way a strike could be won. The strikers would lose working time, with neither strike fund nor unemployment insurance as a buffer, and when the strike was over they would find their jobs permanently filled by braceros.

Galarza resolved this moral dilemma in the only way his conscience would permit.

"I made up my mind that, until the law was changed, I would never again ask a farm worker to stick his neck out where it could be chopped off by one stroke of the pen—a pen held in the hand of some bureaucrat in San Francisco or Washington, D.C.—certifying more braceros. For me to ask farm workers to go out on demonstration strikes that they could not possibly win would have been using them for other purposes. I would rather see the union die than use human beings in that way.

"Now, if a group of workers asked me to come in and said they had already made up their minds they wanted to walk off the job, and wanted my advice, the situation was different. I would tell them, in full detail, the consequences of what they were doing, as I saw them. If they still insisted, I would give them all the assistance I could. There were situations like this now and then. The workers always lost, but there are times when men grow so desperate they would rather take actions they know will lose, than to continue to endure the unendurable."

Galarza consistently personalized his opposition, a technique which was not widely understood or accepted even by his friends. Unlike Father McCullough, he did not believe it was enough to belabor an abstraction, such as the "evil bracero system." In order to educate farm workers, and to arouse the general public, Galarza believed it was necessary to translate the abstractions into real acts by real individuals. Whenever he spoke of the abuses of the system, therefore, he tried to use as an illustration a specific bracero or a specific domestic worker who had undergone a specific type of treatment at the hands of a specific foreman or other official at a specific ranch on a specific date. Beyond that, he tried always to trace the abuses to the ultimate seats of responsibility: he named names of state and federal administrators he considered particularly culpable.

Unlike some critics of the system, Galarza did not believe that the bracero program was inherently unadministrable. Elimination of the program was the goal, but as long as it remained on the books he felt there was much latitude for administrators to make it better or worse. Convinced that administrators were systematically using this latitude to the detriment of agricultural workers, he reserved for these men a contempt beyond anything he felt toward growers, merchants, chiseling doctors, insurance companies, pushers, drivers, labor contractors, and others who took advantage of the helplessness of farm workers in general and braceros in particular. Although he despised it, he could understand the behavior of an agribusinessman whose motive was frankly to make as much money as possible. But he could not understand the public servants whose salaries were paid by American taxpayers, whose duty, by law, was to protect and advance the interests of American workers, but who (so it seemed to Galarza) betrayed their duty, not for money, but for the sake of betrayal itself.

Among the public officials he considered particularly responsible for the maladministration of the bracero system, Galarza identified Robert Goodwin, Director of the U.S. Bureau of Employment Security; Don Larin, Chief of the BES Farm Placement Service and later the California Department of Employment's highest farm labor official; Glenn Brockway, BES Administrator for the Western states; and Edward Hayes, head of the California Farm Placement Service. Hayes resigned in 1960, after the state Attorney General's office proved Farm Placement representatives had been discriminating against domestic workers and accepting gratuities from bracero users. He immediately became chief executive of the Imperial Valley Farmers Association, one of the nation's largest bracero-user groups.

Among those who have manipulated the fate of farm workers over the years, there is a game with generally well-understood rules. Heads of government agencies who administer foreign and domestic farm worker recruitment programs, and heads of labor groups who ritually criticize these programs, have far more in common with each other than either group has with agricultural workers. Within the rules of the game, it is tacitly understood that, whatever public pronouncements may be called for by the role of one or the other, there are no serious animosities, and it is bad form to hold a grudge. Established trade unions and the Department of Labor have a symbiotic relationship and neither is going to jeopardize it over an issue as peripheral to their traditional interests as farm labor.

Galarza understood this minuet, was repelled by it, and refused to dance to it. The following reminiscence is characteristic:

". . . I attended one of these conferences with state and federal people. You know the type. 'We're all interested in basically the same things here. Let's be reasonable.' The chairman was some unctuous bum who had made a career out of knifing farm workers in general and our union in particular. In a polite way, of course. He looked around the table and said, 'We can be on a first-name basis here. You call me So-and-so, and I'll call you Ernesto.' I said to him, 'You are quite mistaken, Mr. Chairman. I will call you Mister So-and-so, and you will call me *Mister* Galarza.' "

The players of the game did not know how to deal with someone who refused to play by their rules. In the end, they had to choose between radically rethinking their assumptions or ejecting this maverick from the game. They chose to eject Ernesto Galarza, and had no trouble constructing justifications which they found entirely convincing.

Galarza fought back. As his personification of the opposition grew more refractory and his attacks more envenomed, some of his friends were unable to follow him. It seemed to them that his attacks were assuming the aspect of a vendetta. Galarza denied that it was a matter of personalities: "I may want to destroy a man's power in certain areas, but not the man himself. . . . It would be absurd for me to hound a person after he was removed from the kind of position in which he could make decisions harming farm workers."

From time to time, the president of the NAWU, H. L. Mitchell, whose headquarters were in Washington, D.C., asked Galarza to modify his attacks on government officials and labor bureaucrats: "After all, Ernie, I have to work with these guys back here." But Galarza felt that his candor made it easier for Mitchell to function: "Let me be the one they hate, Mitch. By comparison with me, you will be a model of sweet reasonableness."

The bracero program's administrators developed a standard tactic of turning the barbs back upon Galarza. In a radio interview in February, 1959, for instance, Secretary of Labor James Mitchell exemplified this technique: "Galarza is an able person and I may agree with some of his objectives, but he hurts his own cause with his extreme, unfounded allegations." Labor leaders who were stung by Galarza's shafts picked up the same patronizing line: "Too bad about Galarza . . ."

Galarza continued to believe that his technique of trying to pinpoint responsibility for the bracero system was a sound use of his limited time and resources. But subsequent events showed that the system had a momentum of its own, sufficient to carry along with it anyone who might be in a given administrative position at a given moment. When Edward Hayes was removed from his key position, the newly elected governor, Pat Brown, put "liberals" in charge of the California Department of Employment and its farm labor functions. Yet, throughout Brown's eight years in office, braceros remained in California. During the last two of those years, California was the only state in the Union to import any braceros at all.

Galarza's enemies carefully cultivated the legend that he was "Mr. Farm Labor"—that the farm labor movement began and ended with him—in the belief that if they could destroy his reputation the movement itself would be destroyed. One of their gambits was to smear him as a Communist. Galarza declined to honor this calumny with any reply. He assumed that his record would speak for itself. Throughout his adult life, he had been fighting all forms of totalitarianism, not with empty words, but by building democratic structures. He confided to a friend, almost in bewilderment, "Can't they see? I love this country in a way that people don't if they are born here, and take it for granted, and have never seen what things are like anywhere else. I love this country because, for all the things wrong, it comes close—close enough to glimpse what the good society might be like. The best way I can possibly imagine to show my respect and affection is to come closer yet—to help get over that remaining gap."

So long as the red-baiting was directed solely at him, Galarza remained silent. But when his wife was drawn into the smears, Galarza's chivalry and family pride compelled him to take steps.

After teaching in the San Jose school system for nearly three years, Mae Galarza was abruptly told that her contract would not be renewed. Suspecting pressure from local growers, Galarza demanded the right to inspect his wife's personnel file. In the course of the controversy, the superintendent of the school district publicly called Galarza a "Red." Galarza brought suit, in one of the first actions of its kind; this was at the time Joseph McCarthy was still riding high. Galarza won the case. Although only token damages were awarded, the message was apparently passed along the growers' network. Ernesto and Mae Galarza were not publicly attacked in this particular way again. But Mrs. Galarza's job in the San Jose schools was never restored.

It would be an exaggeration to say that Galarza stood entirely alone during the middle 1950's. He had friends; he could not have done the things he did without their help. He had friends in a Joint U.S.–Mexico Trade Union Committee, which included representatives of the AFL, the CIO, the independent United Mine Workers, and various railroad brotherhoods. He also had friends in the Fund for the Republic. Late in 1955, Galarza received a grant-in-aid from the Fund to write a report on the bracero system. For four months he gathered evidence, from the impoverished villages of Mexico to the rich fields and orchards of California.

A report of several hundred pages, illustrated by scores of photographs, was submitted to the Fund for the Republic. With the help of John Cogley, former editor of *Commonweal,* Galarza condensed this material into an eighty-page booklet, and in July, 1956, *Strangers in Our Fields* was published by the Joint U.S.–Mexico Trade Union Committee. It was the most damaging bombshell to hit the institution of braceroism up to that time.

The institution was hurt. There is no other way to explain the way in which its functionaries reacted. Rather than ignoring the report, as they had ignored other criticisms, they ordered field representatives of the California Farm Placement Service to search for evidence to discredit Galarza. This enterprise probably cost tens of thousands of tax dollars. The quibbles were sent to Ed Hayes and through him to Glenn Brockway. In August, the San Francisco regional office of the Bureau of Employment Security mimeographed a long critique of *Strangers in Our Fields,* with every intention of making it public. At the last minute, however, Department of Labor officials in Washington concluded that it would be the better part of valor not to joust with Galarza openly.

In his field work, careful as he might be, Galarza was not always able to avoid receiving misinformation. For instance, he unearthed some check stubs which appeared to show that a bracero working for the Southern California Farmers Association had net earnings of $6.48, $6.03, and $2.88 for three consecutive weeks' work. These stubs were reproduced in the booklet, over a quote from one of Galarza's interviews with a bracero: "You work one day, and another —no. We spent much time counting the flies, as the saying is."

The government agencies had access to payroll records; Galarza did not. They found he had been misinformed. Each of the checks was for one *day's* work. With this and a handful of other discrepancies, the agencies sought to bring the entire work into disrepute and to paint its author as a shoddy researcher at best and perhaps even a deliberate liar.

As anyone walking through a bracero camp with his eyes open could have verified, braceros did indeed spend "much time counting the flies." For that matter, it is difficult to see how $2.88 for a full day's work is much more defensible than $2.88 for a week's work. By keeping the argument on their own terms, however, proponents of the system were able to persuade themselves and some innocent by-standers that Galarza was irresponsible.

Actually, much of Galarza's treatment of the bracero system, then and later, was understated. In *Strangers in Our Fields,* he said almost nothing about "health insurance" which constituted one of the system's major rackets; almost nothing about the subsystem of so-called "specials" under which Lyndon Johnson and other favored employers were able to obtain "predesignated" braceros.

Galarza was fully aware of the need for factual accuracy and careful documentation. He knew that proponents of the system placed all the burden of proof on its critics. He knew that they would search exhaustively for some trivial misstatement in order to bring a carefully built edifice of research tumbling down. Even a professionally trained researcher like Galarza found it almost impossible to prove a charge against the bracero system beyond any cavil. Employers' records were closed to him. Wage and hour data were altered. Potential witnesses were hustled back to Mexico.

Nevertheless, *Strangers in Our Fields* proved one of the outstanding successes of Galarza's career. It received widespread publicity, even in media, such as the Los Angeles *Times,* which no one had ever accused of pro-labor prejudice. The booklet went through two editions and 10,000 copies. Condensations of much the same material appeared in at least three national magazines. Urban liberals were slowly being weaned from the misconception that the "farm labor problem" in California was still a matter of jalopies, and Joad families played by Jane Darwell and Henry Fonda.

Galarza's booklet also helped stir into wakefulness some elements of the labor movement. Early in 1957, the AFL-CIO's Industrial Union Department, headed by Walter Reuther, gave the National Agricultural Workers Union $25,000, with the understanding that about half of it would be used for organizing in California.

Pitiable as the amount was, this was the most money Galarza had ever had to work with. Husbanding it carefully, he made it last over a year. He opened offices, sometimes rent-free in private homes, in Yuba City, Tracy, Stockton, Modesto, Hollister, and San Jose and began to "develop local people." As he later put it: "Obviously, you aren't going to organize a statewide union with that kind of money. I looked upon it as a demonstration project. . . . I wanted to prove that Galarza wasn't the only potential organizer in California. Over the years, I would estimate that I have found at least two hundred people in this state—field workers—who would be first-rate organizers, given the chance."

The key problem facing Galarza was this: around what axis can you organize, when your members' jobs will almost certainly be filled by braceros if they try to rise above the braceros' wages and working conditions? To an extent, Galarza answered this question in the same way as Father McCullough and Cesar Chavez, although there was little exchange of ideas among the three. The union proved its value to its members by performing services they lacked the time or expertise to perform, and which did not involve a premature collision with employers. For instance, Galarza's San Jose local discovered that, although agricultural workers had become partially covered by the Social Security Act in 1955, growers and labor contractors often pocketed the payroll deductions rather than sending them to the Social Security Administration. One union member who had worked for a single employer all year, and had earned close to $2,400, was credited with only $427 by the SSA accounting office in Baltimore. A union representative was able to get the "error" corrected.

Galarza felt that an NAWU local should also perform a quite different type of function. In effect, he trained his cadres to operate as he himself was operating: as sleuths for abuses under the bracero program. He was still convinced that there was little point in ordinary union activities as long as Public Law 78 was intact, and that the best way to obtain its modification was to ferret out the most flagrant scandals and publicize them.

In August, 1957, Galarza was sure he had a case which would "blow the whole thing out of the water." Thousands of American fruit pickers were gathering in the northern end of the Sacramento Valley, around Marysville and Yuba City, in anticipation of the peach harvest. Due to unseasonably cold weather, the peaches ripened late. While waiting, the Americans looked for jobs as box-spreaders, limb-proppers, and whatever else might be available in the area. They found all such work being done by braceros, although this was contrary to the letter of the braceros' contracts and to the spirit of Public Law 78.

Galarza had complained of this type of violation on many other occasions, only to be told in so many words, "Oh, really? Prove it." Under this peculiar institution the standards of evidence required of critics of the system would have taxed a Blackstone, but Galarza gleefully accepted the challenge on this occasion, because he felt the evidence was irrefutable. Accompanied by a notary public, he went along the ditch banks and under the bridges of Sutter and Yuba counties, and obtained nearly two hundred sworn affidavits, complete with names, dates, places, every detail, from American workers who had vainly sought employment in the pre-harvest period. The northern California press carried the story as front-page news for days. Galarza called for a withdrawal of braceros, and for an investigation of the entire Farm Placement Service.

Governor Goodwin J. Knight rode out the storm, saying that the state Department of Employment, parent agency of the Farm Placement Service, should "be given an opportunity to look over the situation." By the time the Director of Employment had conducted his "investigation," exonerated himself and his department, and declared Galarza's charges "completely without merit," the peach harvest was half finished, American pickers were either working or had drifted from the area, the media no longer considered the incident newsworthy, and Galarza's salvos were bursting in air unseen and unheard.

Galarza began writing a series of open letters to the Governor on the bracero scandal-of-the-week. He called them his "Knight letters." It is doubtful that the Governor ever read them; the letters were intended primarily for newsmen, church and political groups, and friends of the farm labor movement.

When Democratic victories in the 1958 elections ended the public career of Goodwin Knight, Galarza turned to writing straight press releases on the endless irregularities he and his representatives were uncovering in the field. A typical release began: "Death took a turn as compliance officer for the Department of Labor in Imperial Valley, pointing a bony finger at one more routine violation of Public Law 78 . . ." A bracero had been killed while driving a tractor, an activity prohibited under the master contract, but commonplace. The Department of Labor, in "an indecently hasty whitewash," alleged that the bracero was operating the tractor only "as a special favor" to the regular driver, and as a consequence there was no violation. Galarza demanded a full investigation at once, "before the truth is lost forever under a cloud of malathion and bureaucratic servility." As usual, his eloquence was ignored.

In time, weary of researching, writing, mimeographing, and distributing releases which were seldom if ever used, Galarza turned to writing essays which were apparently more for his own pleasure than anything else, although he distributed them to a small circle of friends. These essays are worth reading not only for their content but for their sardonic wit and verbal felicities. In a representative example of the Galarza style, he characterized the government's disciplinary measures against violators of Public Law 78 as "ten lashes laid on with a half-cooked noodle."

An essay entitled "Labor's Back Yard" is especially significant. Galarza charged that labor leaders "offer only token opposition while [their] most solemn pledges on human decency and democracy are denied one large segment of the brotherhood of labor." In conclusion, he warned:

> If democracy, freedom of organization and collective bargaining are principles, they apply to all. The struggle to realize them must be pressed into every corner of the land, their enjoyment denied no worker, however destitute or ignorant he may be.
>
> Otherwise, labor's long, bitter and often tragic commitment to humanity becomes a game of odd-man-out. The odd man must always be the low man on the totem pole. Once the "right to work" men have laid the axe to the base . . . no trade unionist need ask: "For whom does the axe fall?" It falls for him.

Galarza's near-despair was understandable. He exhausted the small grant from the Industrial Union Department early in 1958. He prepared a careful proposal to the IUD, calling for $250,000. With that amount, he was sure he could build a self-sustaining agricultural workers' union in California. He said later, "They didn't even have the courtesy to reply. For eight months I waited. I made three trips to Washington, trying to build a fire under them. I had to close some union offices, disband some locals, and borrow $3,000 from friends to keep the others going."

The principal reason for the mysterious silence from Washington was that wheels were beginning to turn at the highest echelons of the national AFL-CIO, with motive power altogether different from Galarza's $250,000 program. The decision-makers involved did not feel it necessary to seek the advice of the one man who had had most experience organizing agricultural workers in California, or even to notify him that plans were under way. Convinced that farm labor had been forgotten, Galarza became increasingly caustic in his comments about the California Labor Federation and the national AFL-CIO. In one of his gentler anecdotes, he said:

"Why is it that labor fakers always look so well fed? One time I was at a meeting with three or four of them. It was at one of these plush motels. It would be beneath their dignity to gather in a workingman's place. There they were, around the pool, overflowing their swimming trunks, wallowing around in the water for all the world like a bunch of great white whales. I felt like Captain Ahab making the discovery of his life! If I had had a harpoon handy, I would not like to be responsible for what might have happened."

Galarza's verbal harpoons helped to ensure that when the plans of the national leadership were completed he would be denied any significant role in them.

In February and March, 1959, when Jack Livingston, AFL-CIO Director of Organization, was looking for someone to head the new Agricultural Workers Organizing Committee, Galarza was never seriously considered. To the extent that his name arose at all, the decision-makers in Washington invoked the usual incantation, "Too bad, but he's lost his effectiveness." The most logical choice for the directorship of the Agricultural Workers Organizing Committee was, with only H. L. Mitchell's voice raised in his behalf, bypassed in favor of Livingston's old crony, Norman Smith.

The situation was as unfair to Smith as it was to Galarza, but each tried in good faith to make the best of it. In AWOC's early days, many magazines and newspapers assigned reporters to the story of "Big Labor's all-out drive in agriculture." Many reporters went first to Galarza; he invariably referred them to Smith. For all the general public might have divined from the resulting stories, the organizing drive was a one-man undertaking, with Norman Smith as the new "Mr. Farm Labor."

Giving the lie to those who said he was a "prima donna," constitutionally incapable of "playing on a team," Galarza functioned as a training officer for AWOC. Each day, he traveled to a different area—Stockton, Modesto, Hollister, Yuba City, other far-flung points —to preside at a staff meeting of local organizers and stewards, asking and answering questions, anticipating problems likely to arise in the field.

As time passed, it became clear to Galarza that Smith was strategically adrift, with no coherent idea of how agricultural workers might be organized. In addition, Galarza believed that Smith was wrong in many tactical details, such as a tendency to rely on the assurances of politicians, while Galarza mistrusted all of them. But he held his peace. The staff meetings continued through December, although in the absence of any organizing plan it became increasingly difficult to train a staff. The break came in January, 1960, precipitated by jurisdictional and philosophical problems which had long been simmering in the farm labor movement.

Norman Smith used to say in all seriousness, "I don't care if the Devil himself comes to earth to organize farm workers, as long as the job gets done." Although he might have drawn the line at the Devil, Father McCullough also subscribed to this general theory, on the assumption that even if the union were initially undemocratic or otherwise unsavory, it could later be reformed from within.

Ernesto Galarza did not accept the proposition that any farm labor union at all is preferable to none. Both principled and practical considerations influenced his position. The only proper objective of the labor movement, he felt, is "the kind of human being it produces." He was not interested in the kind of union which produces dependent, manipulable people, even if they are well paid and well fed. He was interested in a union which would help people become more autonomous, more responsible, better able to weigh alternatives and make decisions for themselves. He feared that such a potential for human development would be lost if farm workers were absorbed by some larger union.

At the more "practical" level, Galarza doubted that a merger of agricultural workers with any other union would serve even to "put pork chops on the table." He had long since concluded that established union leaders, no matter how sincerely they might try, could not think within a framework which was relevant to farm workers' problems. "Organized labor just doesn't have any answers to questions like 'What do you do about braceros?' " he pointed out, "because it has never had to deal with foreign contract labor in any other union."

Galarza could not resist noting, furthermore:

"There is no love for the NAWU in the labor movement. We are an embarrassing stepchild. We embarrass them simply by existing. We are a constant reminder to them of things they should have done, but did not do. . . .

"And I'll tell you another way we stand to embarrass the fakers. . . . If we succeed, we'll precipitate a political crisis in the State of California. There'll hardly be a politician in the state who'll be safe. We were instrumental in electing the first Mexican-American council-man in the history of Brawley when we were active in that area. We have upset well-entrenched regimes in the Arvin-Lamont area of Kern County and in Sutter County. And this was done on peanuts.

"If the AFL-CIO gives us the support we have been crying for all these years, we can stand the State of California on its ear. Naturally, this makes a lot of people nervous. Very nervous. Including a lot of people in the labor movement, who have worked out some very careful living arrangements with incumbents—in both parties."

Fairly early in the history of AWOC, Galarza and H. L. Mitchell began to suspect that AFL-CIO officials were bent on dismantling the NAWU in favor of the United Packinghouse Workers of America. In their efforts to preserve what they considered the legal and moral jurisdiction of the NAWU, Galarza and Mitchell said and did things which some observers interpreted as an attempt to bring down the whole farm labor movement in a general Götterdämmerung. Such an interpretation was as superficial as it was uncharitable. Some personal feelings were involved, to be sure. Galarza and Mitchell would have had to be immune to normal human emotion if, after holding the fort so long, they had felt no resentment at being elbowed aside by Johnny-come-latelies. Basically, however, they fought to preserve the jurisdiction of the NAWU because they felt it alone represented the best interests of agricultural field workers. They had serious misgivings about the political backgrounds of some UPWA leaders. But they would have been equally reluctant to see farm workers delivered into the hands of Teamster leaders whose politics were at the other end of the spectrum.

In an attempt to retain the integrity of the NAWU, Galarza and Mitchell clawed with a tenacity which some friends of the farm labor movement, particularly in the Eastern "liberal establishment," could not understand. These friends of the movement supported the vague ideal of a farm labor union; to Galarza, an ideal which was vague was not good enough.

He had sworn an oath of allegiance to his tiny, quixotic union of Anglo, Mexican, and Negro sharecroppers, tenant farmers, and day laborers:

> [I shall] do all in my power to promote the best interest of the Union. I shall never by word or deed do anything that may be harmful to a fellow worker. I promise to go to the aid of my fellow Union worker in time of need, even at the risk of my life. . . .

Galarza felt it would be a violation of this oath—it would be "harmful to a fellow worker"—if he acquiesced passively as the NAWU jurisdiction was taken over by AWOC or UPWA. In the end, the STFU-NFLU-NAWU went out of existence after more than twenty-five years as an independent entity. But at least it set the terms: the Amalgamated Meatcutters and Butcher Workmen of North America created an agricultural department, honored all of NAWU's pension plans and other obligations to its members, and hired Mitchell and Galarza as farm labor organizers.

Galarza chafed under the various forms of "moderation" imposed by an established international union, and an old AFL craft union at that. He criticized Meatcutters' officials whom he regarded, in his phrase, as "all starch and no linen." Such criticism doubtless found its way back to their ears. Although Mitchell has continued on the Meatcutters' payroll and has had some success organizing in Louisiana, Galarza resigned after a few months. He was again "at liberty."

Expenses on his unpretentious home in San Jose are lower than average, and he and his wife meet a large proportion of their food needs from a backyard garden which they tend expertly and affectionately. When he said at the end of 1962, "This has been my least encouraging year," he was referring not to the financial pinch but to the psychological pinch. He was almost a forgotten man; the farm labor movement was almost a forgotten movement. AWOC had become a travesty. There seemed no prospect that the bracero system would ever end. Galarza was writing a book, but could not find a commercial publisher who considered the subject of braceroism important.

Something of a renascence of the farm labor movement, and of Galarza's career within that movement, took place in 1963. On May 29, the House of Representatives unexpectedly voted to discontinue the bracero program. Although the action was rescinded a few months later, it was a serious blow to the aura of invincibility which Public Law 78 had long enjoyed, and it counteracted some of the despair into which many of the friends of farm labor had sunk.

Then, on September 17, the California farm labor movement was electrified, and the gloaming of braceroism was hastened, by the bloodiest in a long series of catastrophes traceable to the insensitive way in which foreign contract-labor gangs had always been handled. In this case, the driver of a rudely converted truck full of braceros drove into the path of a speeding Southern Pacific freight train near the tiny town of Chualar in the Salinas Valley. Thirty-two of the workers were killed.

The old fires flared again in Ernesto Galarza. It was the kind of scandal he had long believed could be used as the springboard for a full-scale Congressional investigation, which in turn might disgrace the bracero program's administrators and sound the death knell of the entire system. His cries for an official investigation had never come to fruition, but now he roused himself for a last effort. Bringing into play all his skills of speaking, writing, flattering, badgering, maneuvering, he persuaded the large Mexican-American population of San Jose to back him solidly in asking the House of Representatives Committee on Education and Labor to investigate the Chualar disaster and to appoint him as staff director.

In some respects, Galarza's luck was good, in others, bad. Fortune, in both cases, revolved around the personality of the chairman of the Education and Labor Committee, Adam Clayton Powell. A more politic chairman would not have hired the "controversial" Galarza in the first place, or kept him on in the teeth of the gale which his appointment aroused. Congressman Charles Gubser, a grower and a major user of braceros, had represented Galarza's district for some years. Protected by Congressional immunity, Gubser took to the floor of the House with unprecedented personal attacks on both Ernesto and Mae Galarza. Ignoring the opposition, Powell told Galarza to proceed with his report and let the chips fall where they might. The report appeared in the spring of 1964: one of the most thoroughly researched and best-written reports ever to appear under the imprimatur of a committee of the United States Congress.

At this point, however, it became evident that Powell's commitment to agricultural labor was no more than skin-deep. There was no follow-up to any of Galarza's recommendations in terms of legislation, although in its documentation of employer negligence the report was useful to attorneys for the survivors of the dead braceros. Instead of the settlements of $1,000 to $1,500 which had initially been made, settlements totaling over $2 million were eventually obtained.

Powell's lack of any real interest in agricultural labor also worked against the realization of a dream Galarza had entertained for years. He was not given the authority to put under subpoena his old enemies, ask them the questions they had always ignored or evaded, and require them to answer publicly from the witness stand under penalty of perjury. About a year later, though, acting on his own with the assistance of a volunteer attorney, James Murray, Galarza came close to realizing this long-standing desire.

The Di Giorgio Corporation, in 1960, had sued a number of AWOC officials for showing the old film, "Poverty in the Valley of Plenty," which allegedly libeled the corporation. Galarza had been named a defendant, although he not only had had nothing to do with the showing but was not even associated with AWOC at that time. Galarza filed a countersuit, claiming malicious prosecution. In the course of this countersuit, he and Murray were able to obtain a number of depositions revealing interconnections between agricultural corporations and the government agencies which supposedly regulated them.

The verdict, rendered late in 1964, was another partial victory or partial defeat, depending on the perspective. The jury found that Galarza had had nothing to do with the showing of the allegedly libelous film, but it awarded him none of the damages he had asked.

Galarza retired to his writing, completing his analysis of the bracero system, for which Alaska Senator Ernest Gruening, an old friend, wrote the foreword. As its title implies, *Merchants of Labor* is an account of that portion of the agribusiness complex which deals in workers, rather than growing or selling fruits and vegetables. In particular, it is the story of bracero-user associations and the government administrators who catered to them. Although 1964 was the climactic year in the political struggle over Public Law 78, publishers still considered Galarza's book "uncommercial." He borrowed $1,500, paid to have this book printed by a San Jose firm, and undertook his own publicity and distribution. Orders came in; the first printing was sold out. In time, there was a second printing.

Then things were quiet again. By now there was a definite economic as well as psychological pinch. With many a wry comment, Galarza found a job with the War on Poverty. It required that he move to Los Angeles, but he did not give up the house in San Jose. In a little more than a year he was back, living on savings again, free to say what he pleased on any subject.

He is in some demand as a consultant—to the Ford Foundation, for instance, on a project having to do with Mexican-Americans in the Southwest. He appears frequently as a speaker at "brown power" conferences, where increasingly politically conscious Mexican-Americans are attempting to formulate a philosophy and program around which they can rally. He has published another book, entitled *Spiders in the House and Workers in the Field*, dealing with the 1947–1950 strike against Di Giorgio, and its aftermaths—including the part played by then Congressman Richard Nixon.

Galarza's contact with the farm labor movement is now minimal. He has no illusions about returning to the movement in which he invested so much of his life. In January, 1967, he journeyed to Delano, but came back to report that Cesar Chavez was too busy to see him. Other times, other leaders: that is the way of social movements. Ernesto Galarza—fiery, loyal, brilliant, proud, organizer and doctor of philosophy—would no doubt agree.

7. The Organizer:
Cesar Chavez (Part 1)

Leadership of an effective social movement need not necessarily arise from the persons most likely to benefit from it. Primary leadership of the abolition movement did not and could not come from slaves. Leadership of the child labor movement did not and could not come from children.

During most of the history of the farm labor movement in California, primary leadership did not come from the isolated, semicaptive groups which made up the agricultural work force. Leadership came from political groups (such as the IWW), urban unionists (Norman Smith, Clive Knowles), intellectuals (Ernesto Galarza), the clergy (Thomas McCullough), and sometimes even from representatives of foreign governments (Carlos Ariza).

There is a fine justice, however, when leadership is assumed by a person who is himself from the aggrieved group and has never really left it. That has now occurred in the farm labor movement in California. It has achieved its greatest successes under the leadership of Cesar Chavez. (The correct pronunciation is, phonetically, Sehssar Tchahvez, with accents on the first syllables.) Chavez is a Chicano (Mexican-American) who worked in the fields as he organized; who looks and talks and acts as farm workers do; who is trusted by farm workers as perhaps no other leader of the movement has ever been.

The Chavez clan, headed by Cesar's grandparents, came to the United States as refugees from the Mexican revolution. Joining other displaced persons, they moved across the Southwest with the crops, but unlike most of the others, they were able to save enough to make a down payment on a farm of their own near the Colorado River in Arizona. There, in 1927, Cesar Estrada Chavez was born. His father's name, Librado, means Freedom.

The Chavez family managed to hold its land through most of the Depression, yielding only in 1938 to the combination of forces arrayed against small landowners. Migrants again, they started west, unprepared for the viciousness which California's farm labor jungle had assumed during the Depression.

For the next several years, they lived in their car, or in tents without heat or light; went without shoes in the winter; ate wild mustard greens to stay alive; were used mercilessly by labor contractors. In time, the family learned the tricks of labor contractors, learned where to find work, how long to stay, when to move on.

Cesar Chavez does not recall these memories bitterly, but matter-of-factly, and often with self-deprecatory humor. This style, and the memories themselves, are significant elements in his leadership of the Spanish-speaking farm workers of the Southwest. Virtually every farm laborer has had similar experiences—experiences beyond the full comprehension of urban-dwellers who, no matter how poor, enjoy protections of the quasi-welfare state which are denied farm workers.

Urban friends of the farm labor movement sometimes find it difficult to understand that the workers do not want pity and do not expend it on themselves. Chavez unerringly captures the right tone when he finds something absurd in the situation: when he turns it back upon himself, and rather than crying, "What pigs labor contractors are!" says, with a weary smile, "Boy, were we green!"

Like other migrant children, Cesar had to change schools several times each year, as his parents moved with the crops. The inadequacies of his education were compounded by the general substandardness of rural schools and by the traditional shunting of Spanish-speaking migrant children into segregated classrooms which provided little more than a child care service. Nevertheless, Chavez had completed the eighth grade by the time he was fourteen and had to leave school to work full-time in the fields.

In his early twenties, he married Helen Favila, daughter of a *zapatista* hero of the Mexican revolution. In 1949, the first of eight children was born to Cesar and Helen Chavez. Like most second-generation Mexican-Americans, they left the migrant stream, settling in San Jose, where Cesar worked in apricots and other local crops. During the off-season, he took whatever odd jobs he could find, such as lumber-stacking. In time, he would no doubt have left agricultural work altogether, but the farm labor movement changed his life—as he, in turn, was to change the farm labor movement.

The seed of farm worker organizing was planted early in Cesar Chavez. When he was about twelve, there was an insurgency within the Dried Fruit and Nut Packers Union of the AFL. Most of the members, including Cesar's father and uncle, wanted to affiliate with the CIO instead. During the controversy, young Cesar listened to their talk about the merits and demerits of various forms of unionism. Eventually, Warehousemen's Local No. 6 of the CIO won the dispute. Librado Chavez supported many other organizing efforts while his son watched and listened and learned.

Cesar showed, quite early in his life, that he had an independent spirit, and deep convictions about justice. In 1943, when he was fifteen, he was expelled from a Delano motion picture theater for refusing to conform to the practice of segregated seating. When the National Farm Labor Union began organizing in the lower San Joaquin Valley in the late 1940's, Cesar joined, marched in picket lines, and remained a member for several years.

After his marriage, he lived in the same town as Ernesto Galarza, but their paths rarely crossed. When the full fire was struck in the breast of Cesar Chavez, it was from another flint.

Cesar and Helen Chavez lived on the east side of San Jose, on the "wrong side" of Highway 101. The area was known among its inhabitants, with representative Mexican humor, as Sal Si Puedes, which means "Get out if you can." At about this time, Father Donald McDonnell was building a mission in Sal Si Puedes, naming it after Our Lady of Guadalupe. The Virgin of Guadalupe, the "Dark Madonna," is an important unifying symbol among Mexicans, even those who are not practicing Catholics. This religious-national symbol was later to figure in Chavez's own organizing.

Night after night, Father McDonnell made the rounds of the barrio, talking with people about their problems, in their own homes. In due course, he knocked on Cesar Chavez's door. It was perhaps the most important single meeting in the history of the farm labor movement. In his book, *Huelga,* Eugene Nelson quotes Chavez's recollection, fifteen years later, of that first meeting.

[Father McDonnell] sat with me past midnight telling me about social justice and the Church's stand on farm labor and reading from the encyclicals of Pope Leo XIII in which he upheld labor unions. I would do anything to get the Father to tell me more about labor history. I began going to the bracero camps with him to help with Mass, to the city jail with him to talk with prisoners, anything to be with him. . . .

When a true teacher and a true student come together, they inspire one another. Father McDonnell, however, had a multitude of other obligations. He could go only so far in preparing Chavez for a role in organizing agricultural workers. Then, in 1952, another crucial meeting took place: this one between Chavez and Fred Ross of the Community Service Organization.

The CSO was an outgrowth of the Industrial Areas Foundation, itself an outgrowth of Saul Alinsky's Back of the Yards movement which organized the lower-middle-class area around the Chicago stockyards in the early 1940's. The core of Alinsky's organizing philosophy is the belief that social change is more basic and lasting if the people affected by problems identify those problems for themselves and band together in interest-groups to deal with them. Alinsky enjoyed titillating friends and foes alike with frequent allusions to "radical" and "revolutionary," but his technique was actually a revolution against nothing so much as the paternalistic social-worker mentality.

Alinsky established the Industrial Areas Foundation to apply his method to situations in which there was an unmistakable call from people who considered themselves ready for organizing assistance. Such a call came from the Mexican-American community in Los Angeles in 1947. Well over 100,000 persons of Mexican descent lived in the city, concentrated in a semislum area, Boyle Heights. They were a despised minority, commonly known to the Anglo majority by a contemptuous epithet, *pachuco*. Police brutality against the Spanish-speaking was even more flagrant, perhaps, than that against Los Angeles' Negroes.

Tony Rios, Edward Roybal, and others formed what they called the Community Service Organization. Its purpose was to serve any member of the community—primarily the Mexican-American community, although at no time was it closed to Negroes, Anglos, or anyone else who cared to join. If a member had a complaint against the police department, needed assistance with immigration papers, or the like, he could get help from the CSO.

CSO asked for a professional organizer, and the Industrial Areas Foundation supplied one: Fred Ross, a young Anglo who quickly mastered the Spanish language. By 1949, Ross had trained so many volunteers, who had organized Boyle Heights so well, that CSO was able to elect Ed Roybal to the Los Angeles City Council, the first Mexican-American ever to hold that position. Later, Roybal became California's first Congressman of Mexican ancestry.

Fred Ross began moving into other parts of California to establish additional CSO chapters. He remained only long enough to make sure the local people were well on the way to meeting their own problems, and then he moved elsewhere. He arrived in San Jose early in 1952.

Chavez yielded to the urgings of Father McDonnell and attended one of Ross's house meetings, reluctantly and skeptically. What could anyone from the big city—and an Anglo at that—know about farm workers? But though Chavez came to scoff, he remained to listen. The things Ross said that evening, and the way he said them, appealed to Chavez because they were so consistent with the things the priest had been saying.

The organizing assumptions which McDonnell had reached intuitively were almost identical to those which the Industrial Areas Foundation had reached pragmatically: no decision-making by outside élites; no demagoguery, bombast, or empty threats; rather, a long series of small meetings in private homes, gradually joining in a larger structure. When the time came for a confrontation with existing institutions, the power would be real, not merely theoretical, and could be channeled overnight into picketing, boycotting, sitting-in, voting the rascals out, or other appropriate forms of action.

It is not true, as has often been alleged, that Chavez was "trained by Alinsky." He got all his training in San Jose, while working as a laborer during the day, and in the evenings going to house meetings with Fred Ross. After Chavez proved his competence and perseverance, Ross offered him a job, at $35 a week, organizing on his own. Chavez accepted, although he felt very "awkward" talking to strangers, and sometimes drove around the block several times before he "got up enough nerve" to preside at a house meeting in a new neighborhood. He retains this natural modesty to the present day.

In 1953, Cesar Chavez became a statewide organizer for the CSO. He traveled to Oakland and southern Alameda County; up and down the San Joaquin Valley; to Oxnard, in Ventura County, where he transformed the Mexican-American colónia from a slack agglomeration of defeated men and women, displaced from the lemon groves by braceros, into a tautly mobilized group which won the jobs back through collective action.

Chavez's organizing skills were so evident that, in 1960, he was appointed General Director of the national CSO. With the help, among others, of Dolores Huerta, who became his principal assistant, he built the CSO to a strength of twenty-two active chapters in California and Arizona.

As a direct result of CSO efforts, two major pieces of legislation were enacted. Old Age Security benefits were extended to first-generation Mexicans even if they had not become naturalized citizens; and the state disability insurance program was extended to agricultural workers. The latter was an important advance even though workers themselves had to pay the premiums through a 1 percent payroll deduction. It was the first social insurance program which required all agricultural employers in the state to report precisely who worked for them, how long, and how much they earned: information basic to the ultimate stabilization of the farm labor market.

Despite such achievements, Chavez began to grow restive in his position. Some CSO leaders felt that the solution to the economic and social problems of Spanish-speaking persons was for them to get out of agricultural employment altogether and turn it over to braceros. Chavez could not have disagreed more. The only solution, he believed, was to end the bracero system and upgrade farm work until it was no longer a badge of inferiority, and no longer something from which people would want to flee to the cities. Chavez felt that farm labor organizing should receive the overwhelming emphasis in CSO's program.

Chavez let it be known that he would have to reconsider his place within CSO if the 1962 convention turned down a rural-oriented organizing program. In order to avoid swaying the delegates to a decision which they might not be prepared to back seriously, he made no speeches. His position was understood well enough. When the convention failed to adopt an all-out farm labor program, Chavez submitted his resignation. He had devoted ten years to the CSO, and he did not make this decision lightly. It was an index of the increasing clarity with which he saw what he had to do with his life.

He turned down other jobs which would have paid several times as much as he had made with CSO. He packed, withdrew from the bank his life savings of about $900, and in April, 1962, with his wife and eight children, drove over the Tehachapi Mountains and up the San Joaquin Valley to the town of Delano. He chose Delano for the simplest of reasons: "My brother lived there, and I knew that at least we wouldn't starve."

With no outside support of any kind, Chavez began to organize agricultural workers. In order to avoid any suggestion that the organization would function immediately as an orthodox trade union, he called it the Farm Workers Association. The name was later changed to National Farm Workers Association, but most FWA members continued to use the earlier name, and that practice is followed here.

Chavez is not a dogmatic man, but he came close to it on one point: support from outside, he was sure, could do more harm than good in the formative stages of a movement. Once, at a time when AWOC had already spent over a quarter of a million dollars, he was asked, "If you were offered $250,000 to organize farm workers, how would you spend it?" "I wouldn't," he replied without hesitation. "I would turn it down. Of course," he laughed, "if you wanted to give me five or ten dollars to buy gas to get out of town, I might take it. But no more than ten dollars!"

Chavez felt that large or even medium-sized financial contributions carry strings which may strangle a young, immature organization, but he did not necessarily extend the same theory to an organization which had firmly charted its own course and proved its own vitality. By the end of 1965, Chavez was accepting substantial financial contributions to FWA and not only were they doing no harm, they were enabling the organization to survive what would otherwise have been fatal circumstances.

Another of Chavez's organizing concepts, which could probably be traced to the influence of Father McDonnell, was the necessity for

147

sacrifice. In much the same spirit, Jack London had said shortly after the 1913 Wheatland Riot, "It is always the things we fight for, bleed for, suffer for, that we care the most for."

Dues in FWA were deliberately set at a level which represented a substantial sacrifice for most farm workers: $3.50 per month. Furthermore, the privileges of membership were limited strictly to those whose dues were current, unlike NAWU, AWOC, and other previous organizations, which had been very lenient about such matters. In an interview, Chavez explained: "When members pay so much, they feel they aren't just hangers-on. They feel they are the important part of the organization—that they have a right to be served. They don't hesitate to write, to call, to ask for things. The idea that they, alone, are paying the salary of the man who is responsible to them is very important."

There were many other mansions in the house of Chavez's organizing philosophy. He scrupulously avoided talk of strikes while the Association was small and had no chance of winning. He avoided mass meetings and other means to quick but evanescent membership increases and enthusiasms. He avoided crisis psychology. He assumed he had time enough, and he used time itself as an organizing tool, to let self-seekers and mere talkers drop away, and to let natural leaders of integrity emerge.

Chavez knew that the stereotype of farm workers' homogeneity was false. He knew that Mexican, Anglo, Filipino, and Negro agricultural laborers were often suspicious of one another. He knew that the concerns of out-of-state migrants were not quite the same as the concerns of in-state migrants, and that neither were the same as the interests of the home guard. He knew that many farm workers were likely, at first, to be apathetic or even antagonistic toward unionization: year-round hands who thought of themselves as part of management; green carders who wanted only to return to Mexico with as much money and little trouble as possible; wetbacks who were subject to deportation if they attracted any attention; wounded, disillusioned veterans of previous organizing drives which had failed; housewives, students, and other casual workers who had no intention of remaining in agriculture.

Chavez knew that farm worker "solidarity" was a dream of old radicals or romantic urban friends of the movement, and that in time of crisis some workers would scab on others. The task of the genuine organizer was not to strive for an impossible unity, but to organize as many as possible of the real farm workers: those who had a serious attachment to agriculture and were most essential to the functioning of the industry.

Every night, fighting his fatigue after working in the fields all day, Chavez went to the homes of this type of worker, explaining the Farm Workers Association, pointing out the short-run kinds of things members could do by working together: they could form a credit union; help one another with workmen's compensation and other quasi-legal problems; get preferential rates on insurance.

Chavez had hoped that the organization would be self-supporting by 1963. Dolores Huerta moved to Delano with her six children (she later had a seventh) and served as FWA general assistant. Chavez thought it reasonable to ask that he and she each be paid $50 a week. There were also telephone bills, gasoline, and other expenses. In the late summer of 1963, Chavez admitted, in a discussion with Father McCullough, that his timetable had not been met. FWA had several hundred members, but dues were not fully sustaining the organization. Cesar was working in the fields, sometimes with the help of his wife and older children, to help meet the bills. "Keep going," advised Father McCullough. Chavez did.

By the middle of 1964, the Association was self-supporting. It had perhaps a thousand dues-paying members, in more than fifty local groups, spread over seven counties. Chavez no longer needed to work in the fields. The primary problem now became one of satisfying the members' desire for accomplishment, without entering into precipitate adventures of the type which had led to the demise of so many earlier farm labor organizations.

FWA took a "militant" position for the first time in May, 1965, when it assisted a rent strike against the Tulare County Housing Authority, to protest rent increases of 40 percent at two farm labor camps with very substandard facilities. In the summer of 1965, there were two small strikes, involving FWA members on horticultural farms. Both won their objectives: wage increases, and the rehiring of members who had been discharged.

Something electric was in the air by late August.

No matter how sound its basic plan, how shrewd its day-to-day tactics, and how great the magnetism of its leaders, the career of every social movement is shaped at many crucial points by historical accidents and by unbelievers who know not what they do. The "Delano movement"—which, after September, 1965, the FWA was often called—began fortuitously, and at critical junctures received help from unlikely sources.

When Public Law 78 ended on December 31, 1964, the U.S. Department of Labor continued to admit braceros to California simply by calling them something else and changing the rules slightly. The 1965 rules required payment of $1.40 an hour. Through this requirement, quite unintentionally, the Department of Labor, never renowned as a fearless friend of the farm labor movement, helped set the stage for events in Delano.

The second major impetus came from the self-organized Filipino workers who had joined AWOC six years earlier, and were never members of FWA at all. The AWOC representative assigned to this Filipino group was Larry Itliong. In 1929, when he was fifteen, Itliong had left his home in the Philippines to come to the United States. He had worked in the fields for some years, then moved into the Northwest fishing and canning industries where he helped organize his compatriots. When he joined the staff of AWOC, he made his headquarters in Delano, which served as "home base" for a sizable number of Filipino agricultural workers.

Table grapes are among the crops in which Filipinos have long specialized. California grapes ripen first in the Coachella Valley each year. There, in May, 1965, fortuitous links began coming together into the start of a long chain.

Coachella Valley growers were told by the Department of Labor that they would have to pay braceros $1.40 an hour. Filipino grape pickers felt they were entitled to the same rate. When they did not receive it, they turned for help to Larry Itliong and AWOC. There was a brief work stoppage. Largely through the leverage of the growers' desire for braceros, the Filipinos won their wage demand.

By September, many of these same workers had moved north to the Delano area, where the table grape season was just beginning.

The growers were offering $1.20 an hour, plus a "bonus" of five cents per man per box. The workers saw no reason why they should get less than they had in the Coachella Valley. Again they turned to AWOC. Registered letters, asking for a meeting, were sent to the ten Delano grower-shippers who employed most Filipino grape workers. The letters were ignored. A majority—some say as many as 90 percent—of the Filipinos walked off their jobs.

From the beginning of the strike on September 8, it was taken for granted that FWA members would not cross the Filipinos' picket lines into the premises of the ten struck grower-shippers. But would they be strikebreaking if they continued picking other grapes in the Delano area? It was a painful dilemma for Chavez and the other FWA leaders. They calculated they were about two years away from being prepared for a major strike. On the other hand, how could they permit themselves to give the appearance of scabbing on another farm workers' organization? They decided to put the question to a vote of the FWA membership.

An emergency meeting was called for September 16, the 145th anniversary of the independence of Mexico from Spain. The largest hall in Delano overflowed, with many members standing outside. Emotions were overflowing, too. When no one voiced any misgivings about extending the strike to all Delano grape growers, Chavez took it upon himself to explain how great the sacrifices would be and how limited were FWA's resources.

Nonetheless, the vote for *la huelga* (the strike) was unanimous. The cries went up: "Viva la huelga!" "Viva la causa!" "Viva Cesar Chavez!"

Grape growers evicted the Filipinos from their camps and imported strikebreakers without informing them that a strike was in progress. The growers doubtless expected the strike would run its course within a few weeks, as had been the case with every strike during AWOC's six-year history. From the day FWA entered the strike, however, there were important differences between this and AWOC-led strikes.

Delano growers found they were dealing, not with traditional labor theories and techniques, but with a "new breed" of farm workers, taking their inspiration from Thoreauvian friends of the movement who refused to be intimidated by laws which they conscientiously considered unjust. The new Thoreauvians included civil rights workers who had gone to jail in defiance of the South's notions of law and order; students who had been challenging the "multiversity"; Reverend Chris Hartmire and other young ministers and priests who believed that true reverence lies in the social gospel.

Growers first tried to crush the new breed by time-tested means. They called on their nearly total control over the Kern County sheriff's department and courts. On October 18, forty-four pickets, including nine clergymen, were arrested for chanting "Huelga" from the side of a public road. Cesar Chavez was arrested for trying to communicate with strikebreakers from a light plane equipped with a loudspeaker. He, Dolores Huerta, and other strike leaders were arrested again and again, and had to devote much of their time and energy to court appearances.

Veteran labor reporters for California's metropolitan newspapers said the strike could not possibly be won. Since collective bargaining laws did not apply to agriculture, it was a naked test of strength, and how could the strength of penniless farm workers compare with that of multimillion-dollar corporations?

Paying no attention to the labor experts, Chavez and the other members of the FWA executive committee invented their own precedents as they went along. They decided to follow the grapes out of the fields and to try to upset the distribution system. FWA representatives traced many grape shipments to terminals in San Francisco, Oakland, Stockton, Los Angeles. Some individual members of the Teamsters respected the FWA picket lines. Members of the International Longshoremen's and Warehousemen's Union refused to load "hot" grapes.

By December, 1965, the FWA staff was comparatively well organized. The sensation-seekers and emotionally unstable volunteers had drifted away or been asked to leave, while those who had proved their reliability remained. Many FWA members had emerged as capable leaders and were serving as picket captains. When a crisis arose which could not be handled by an FWA representative on the spot, and could not await a general membership meeting, decisions were made by a group which included the executive officers of FWA —Chavez, Dolores Huerta, and Gilberto Padilla—and a few of the especially responsible volunteers, such as Jim Drake, an ordained minister from the United Church of Christ, and Wendy Goepel, who dropped out from a career in the California Department of Public Health to devote herself to the farm labor movement.

FWA continued probing, searching, upsetting stale formulations. In mid-December, the quest for new directions yielded an inspiration: a boycott against the products of Schenley Industries, one of the two largest Delano firms. The concept of a consumer boycott had been considered many times in the history of the farm labor movement, and had always been rejected as unworkable. FWA went ahead, undeterred. The movement quickly expanded across the country. Trade unionists, students, and other urban sympathizers who had not been able to come to Delano personally could now assist la huelga in useful ways. FWA representatives were dispatched to most of the major cities in the country to organize and coordinate local boycott groups.

On December 18, 1965, a few days after the boycott began, Walter Reuther came to Delano. He pledged $5,000 a month support from his United Automobile Workers union, and began by handing Itliong and Chavez a check for $10,000, the extra $5,000 being a "Christmas present." Reuther had never visited AWOC, in Stockton, when it might have used his leadership between 1959 and 1962. He evidently sensed that the Delano movement had far different prospects from those of the old AWOC.

In March, 1966, Senator Harrison Williams, Democrat of New Jersey, brought his Subcommittee on Migratory Labor to California for public hearings. The ostensible purpose was to gather testimony on a sheaf of six farm labor bills introduced by Williams, but the practical effect of the hearings was to focus public attention on the Delano grape strike more sharply than ever.

On the final day of the hearings, Senator Robert F. Kennedy lent his full influence to the FWA cause. He told the Kern County sheriff, "I suggest you read the Constitution of the United States before you arrest any more strikers." And Kennedy stated, "If we can get a man on the moon by the end of the 1960's, it seems we should be able to work out collective bargaining for farm workers after talking about it for thirty years." His words were transmitted nationally.

From this public relations triumph, FWA vaulted immediately to another. It seems to have been Chavez's own idea, originally: a march to the state capitol in Sacramento to petition Governor Pat Brown to do something about collective bargaining rights for farm workers.

The idea was explored within the FWA executive group. Why not time the march to arrive on the steps of the capitol on Easter morning, which was about a month away? Someone pointed out that this meant the march would take place during the Lenten season, and ought properly to have an aspect of sacrifice and penitence. Someone else noted that many such processions take place in Mexico during Lent, and are known as *peregrinaciones* or pilgrimages.

Another parallel in Mexican history was brought out. When Mexican reformers have felt the time was ripe, they have issued a *pronunciamento*—their plan for setting things right—which is known thereafter by the name of the town in which it was first promulgated. Thus, there have been Plans of Iguala, Zacatecas, San Luis Potosí, and a Plan of Ayala, issued by Emiliano Zapata in 1911. Why not begin a peregrinación with a Plan of Delano? The resulting pronunciamento, a unique blend of revolutionary and religious appeals, written principally by Luis Valdez, was printed and distributed by the tens of thousands.

The length of the march was more than 230 miles: nearly the same, coincidentally, as Gandhi's Salt March to the sea in 1933. For twenty-five days, the Delano pilgrims marched. Several dozen farm workers walked every step of the way For greater or lesser periods of time, these *originales* were joined by many other farm workers, public officials, churchmen, newspapermen, and California citizens of all types. Each night, the march paused in a farm labor community where hospitality was provided in the homes of local farm workers. There was a nightly rally at which the Plan of Delano was read; *corridas* (ballads) about the strike and the march were sung; El Teatro Campesino, the Farm Workers Theater, presented skits lampooning *esquiroles* (scabs) and *patroncitos* (growers); and everyone had a chance to see Cesar Chavez, limping with blisters.

The Plan of Delano described the movement spreading "like flames across a dry plain." This was not entirely rhetorical. News of the march appeared in the California press for twenty-five consecutive days. It was scarcely possible any longer for a literate person to remain unaware of the Delano movement.

On April 6, just four days before Easter, the line of march was galvanized by news which seemed heaven-sent: Schenley had agreed to recognize FWA and to negotiate a contract covering all Schenley field workers in the Delano area. The boycott had won its objective. On the following day, an even more astounding development was announced. After years of implacable opposition to farm unions, officials of the Di Giorgio Corporation suddenly announced that they were offering representation elections to three groups: FWA, AWOC, and an "Independent Kern-Tulare Farm Workers Association."

At high noon on Easter Sunday, with the banner of the Virgin of Guadalupe extending a benediction over all, more than ten thousand persons stood on the steps and adjacent lawns of the state capitol as the peregrinación reached its triumphant conclusion. Prayers, speeches, songs, pledges of support, cries of *Viva!* filled a three-hour rally.

The uninitiated hailed Di Giorgio's offer of representation elections as the beginning of the end for the open shop in California agriculture, but as a matter of fact it was full of booby traps. For instance, the company proposed to let strikebreakers vote, but not strikers. In several meetings between FWA and company representatives, little progress toward eliminating the booby traps was made. The company accused FWA of bad faith and broke off negotiations. FWA thereupon launched a boycott of Di Giorgio's two most readily identifiable products: Treesweet frozen juices, and S & W canned goods.

The company then played its trump card, announcing that the Teamsters union would make a good representative for its Delano workers, and should be included on the ballot. The Teamsters graciously agreed. On June 22, the company abruptly announced that the election would be held within forty-eight hours, under its own ground rules.

Moving fast, FWA and AWOC obtained a court order prohibiting the unauthorized use of their names on the ballot. Two choices remained: the Teamsters and "no union," with the company urging a vote for the Teamsters. Predictably enough, the Teamsters won, but their victory was something less than overwhelming. Of 732 workers eligible to vote under the company's rules, 9 wrote in the name of FWA, 3 wrote in AWOC, 60 voted for "no union," 281 voted for the Teamsters—but 379 declined to vote at all, which is what FWA and AWOC had urged.

Nevertheless, it was a gloomy hour for Cesar Chavez and his organization. For years, knowledgeable observers of the farm labor movement had said, "If the Teamsters ever decide to get into it, look out." With the exception of a couple of contracts with Salinas Valley lettuce growers in 1961, the Teamsters had always stayed out of the fields. But now it looked as though the Teamsters were staking a claim to field workers, and it looked as though nothing could save FWA.

Cesar Chavez and his associates were not panicked. First, they mobilized pressure on Governor Brown. Brown appointed Ronald Haughton, a nationally respected arbitrator, to investigate the Di Giorgio election. Haughton recommended a new election, under fair and reasonable rules. The next step was to induce Di Giorgio and the Teamsters to accept this recommendation. Clergymen called on Teamster officials of their faith. Brown probably used his personal influence with Robert Di Giorgio, an old schoolmate and friend. The full story may never be known, but by July 16, all parties concerned had agreed to a new election.

Under the new rules, everyone who had worked for Di Giorgio for fifteen days or more since the beginning of the strike was eligible to vote. All these persons were by definition strikebreakers, and might be expected to follow the company's advice of a vote for the Teamsters. Di Giorgio workers who had left their jobs when the strike began were also eligible to vote, but by now they had scattered through the Western states and Mexico, usually without forwarding addresses.

FWA had two practical problems, each of which seemed insuperable: to change the attitudes of company-oriented workers; and to locate former employees dispersed over much of the North American continent. Labor experts predicted, as usual, that FWA could not win and the Teamsters could not lose.

FWA went about its business. Fred Ross, Chavez's mentor from fifteen years before, appeared in Delano and began training dozens of volunteer organizers to go into Di Giorgio camps to talk with strikebreakers. When it came to the former employees, Chavez relied heavily on a method which the experts could not have anticipated, since it was quite outside any orthodox union experience.

Through a many-filamented "grapevine," the message went out, penetrating to truck farms in eastern Washington, cotton empires in Texas, tiny villages on the high plateaus of central Mexico. From mouth to mouth, the message went: "Be in Delano on August 30." "Why?" "I'm not sure, exactly. But Cesar says it's important." That was enough to bring scores of former grape workers back to Delano on the appointed date.

The Teamster campaign was conducted by professionals who did not scruple to use such tactics as red-baiting and race-baiting. FWA replied with some invective of its own—of which "jailbird" and "Judas" were representative—but it had far more meaningful arguments. The contract just signed with Schenley proved that FWA was of tangible benefit to its members. The contract provided a starting wage of $1.75 an hour, compared to the $1.40 which other growers were paying; there was a union hiring hall which ended the abuses of labor contractors; there were provisions for seniority, stewards, paid vacations, and other forms of security and dignity California farm workers had never known before.

On August 22, FWA and AWOC merged into a new entity, known as the United Farm Workers Organizing Committee (UFWOC), AFL-CIO. Cesar Chavez became director; Larry Itliong, assistant director. A few sectarians thought this move indicated Chavez had "sold out" his ideals to Big Labor. In point of fact, the problem of dual unionism had troubled FWA and AWOC from the beginning; a merger would soon have been necessary under any circumstances. In further point of fact, a merger was necessary at this particular time in order to preserve anything at all of FWA and its ideals. Chavez knew that losing to the Teamsters would mean the end of the Delano movement, and he foresaw a loss if the legitimate farm worker vote were split between FWA and AWOC.

As a final point of fact, the terms of the merger were such that Chavez retained complete autonomy in strategic and tactical decision-making, the right to continue using volunteer organizers, and all the other prerogatives he considered essential.

The election campaign neared its close. Teamster representatives sponsored a final rally, with free beer, and promptly at 5:00 P.M., as was their wont, retired to the Stardust Motel, Delano's finest, where they swam in the pool or relaxed in air-conditioned rooms. UFWOC representatives worked until late at night, talking with workers in their homes or in labor camps.

Early in the morning on August 30, farm workers began arriving at the polling places, for the first bona fide representation election in California agriculture. They continued to arrive throughout the day, making farm labor history. The official results were announced on September 2. UFWOC had received 530 votes, the Teamsters, 331; 12 workers preferred no union. Cesar Chavez and his dedicated band of amateurs had won a contest against the largest, richest union in the world in league with one of the largest agricultural corporations.

For generations, growers had claimed that farm workers were not interested in belonging to unions, but they had always been careful not to put this claim to an empirical test. Now, for the first time, it had been put to the test. Over 98 percent of the workers wanted union representation, and of that 98 percent nearly two-thirds preferred representation by a union which was financially incorruptible, non-violent, and sensitive to their own opinions and desires.

Later in 1966, UFWOC won a representation election at the Hourigan-Mosesian-Goldberg company, with 285 votes for the union and 38 for "no union." Through sit-ins, moral and legal pressure, and the threat of a renewed consumer boycott, UFWOC gained the right to an election at Di Giorgio's huge Arvin ranch—the scene of NFLU's bitter strike nearly twenty years earlier. Again, UFWOC won, as it has won every time growers have permitted their mythology to be tested against the real world.

In 1967, the union began winning recognition, negotiations, and contracts through "card checks." When union representatives had pledge cards from a clear majority of a company's field workers, they asked for collective bargaining without the delay and acrimony of a contested election which would only result in a union victory in the end. Through card checks, UFWOC has obtained contracts with some of the major wineries in California, including Gallo, Almadén, Christian Brothers, Paul Masson, and Franzia.

When UFWOC attempted to use a card check at Perelli-Minetti, third largest of the Delano grape kings, however, the Teamsters appeared on the scene again. Teamster "organizers" escorted strike-breakers through UFWOC picket lines. The company signed a contract with the Teamsters, in which workers had had no voice, and the terms of which were substantially inferior to those of UFWOC contracts. Cesar Chavez and his colleagues had no recourse but the techniques which had by now become their trademarks—the only techniques possible, given the absence of labor law and the union's commitment to nonviolence—picketing, boycotting, the pressure of public opinion and moral suasion.

For over ten months, the struggle went on, with UFWOC's nonviolence sorely tested by tactics of the Teamsters and the company. Behind-the-scenes mediation by a Catholic priest, Eugene Boyle, an Episcopal minister, Richard Byfield, and a rabbi, Joseph Glazer, was instrumental in working out a "no raiding" agreement between UFWOC and the Teamsters. The Teamsters union agreed to stop interfering with field workers; UFWOC agreed not to invade canneries, warehouses, and produce markets—which it had never done in the first place.

To this point, UFWOC had undertaken three major boycotts; all had ended in contracts. To Chavez and other UFWOC strategists, it seemed clear that the consumer boycott was the most viable answer, perhaps the only answer, to the singular problems of farm labor organizing: What do you do when you represent a majority of workers and employers still refuse to acknowledge your existence? What do you do when green carders fill your jobs and government agencies refuse to enforce the immigration laws?

Organizers reported that most employees of the Giumarra Vineyard Corporation wanted union representation. Chavez wrote to Joseph Giumarra, asking for a meeting "to work out a method to settle the question of recognition . . ." There was no reply. Other overtures were spurned. Several hundred Giumarra workers voted unanimously to strike. Giumarra flooded his vineyards with green carders. Union efforts to stanch this flood were largely unavailing. UFWOC leaders undertook a fourth consumer boycott, emboldened by the success of their previous three. In August, 1967, the great grape boycott began.

Unlike Schenley, Di Giorgio, and Perelli-Minetti, Giumarra dealt in fresh grapes for the table, with no readily identifiable brand name. Furthermore, he began borrowing labels from other table-grape growers—a tactic of doubtful legality under the 1966 "Truth in

Packaging" Act. To meet this tactic, UFWOC leaders decided they would have to boycott *all* California table grapes. They dispatched their best organizers to the major urban centers of the United States and Canada, and trained new organizers to go to cities which had been untouched in previous boycotts.

Mayors or city councils of Cleveland, Detroit, San Francisco, and other cities endorsed the table-grape boycott. So did the legislature of the entire State of Hawaii. New York City was nearly completely "shut down." The movement became international when the Transport Workers' Federation urged its members in Sweden, England, and elsewhere not to unload California grapes.

All the contenders for the 1968 Democratic presidential nomination supported farm workers' right to collective bargaining, and supported the boycott as a legitimate device to secure that right. Hubert Humphrey, after he won the nomination, met personally with Cesar Chavez.

The boycott has been astonishingly effective, both in terms of public education and in its impact on grape sales. Thousands of tons of grapes have been diverted from table use to wineries. Others have had to be sold on the fresh market at reduced prices. Some have been quietly dumped. Even opponents of the boycott concede that it has been 20 to 25 percent effective: total income to grape growers has been that much less than it would most probably have been without the boycott. In a "conspiracy" suit filed in the summer of 1969, the California table-grape industry claimed that it had already been damaged to the extent of $25 million by that time.

Despite these losses, the industry seemed committed to a stand of "death before dishonor," and seemed to feel that recognition of the union would be the ultimate dishonor. Grape growers retained the services of Whitaker & Baxter for public relations purposes, at a reported fee of $2 million. The growers induced the Department of Defense to increase shipments of grapes to Vietnam from 468,000 pounds in 1967 to 2,167,000 pounds in 1969. They induced the California Board of Agriculture, a public agency, to mount a concerted attack on farm unionism in general and the boycott in particular. They induced Richard Nixon to brand the boycott "illegal" under the terms of the Taft-Hartley Act, although Nixon, as a lawyer, as a member of Congress when the Act was passed, and through his personal involvement in the NFLU–Di Giorgio strike in 1950, was unquestionably aware that agricultural workers are excluded from all the terms of the Act, including its provisions concerning boycotts.

Ronald Reagan replaced Pat Brown as governor in 1967. The grape growers recruited the willing Reagan to serve in effect as honorary chairman of their counterboycott. Reagan announced that he was eating more grapes than ever, attributed his good health and looks to them, and lost no opportunity in his travels about the country to denounce the boycott as illegal, immoral, and fattening.

In the late summer of 1968, Chavez and the union became interested in the issue of pesticides, both from the standpoint of their effects on workers' health and because of the possibility of linking them with the grape boycott. Charges and countercharges flew. The union argued that grapes were reaching consumers' tables with residues of DDT and other "hard" pesticides. The industry, through its favorite spokesman in Washington, Senator George Murphy, Republican of California, claimed that the union had falsified some laboratory results. Senator Murphy was subsequently obliged to retract his accusation.

UFWOC attempted to gain access to reports in the offices of county agricultural commissioners, which would indicate the types of pesticides used on specific crops, at specific times and places. The union was denied access to these documents. Legal tests went against the union at the Superior and Appellate Court levels, even though the state Attorney General's office entered the case in support of UFWOC's contention that the documents were public records. The matter is now on appeal to the state Supreme Court.

In the summer of 1969, a dozen large grape growers from the Coachella and San Joaquin valleys, acknowledging that they were going bankrupt from the boycott, tried to break the impasse and entered into negotiations with UFWOC. If these dozen industry leaders had signed contracts, the rest of the table-grape industry might have found some way to save face and recognize UFWOC, too. On July 3, however, the negotiations were adjourned as "hopelessly deadlocked." There were differences on wages, but the principal reason for the deadlock was that UFWOC insisted on pesticide protections which the growers equally adamantly refused to grant.

Many friends of the movement considered the union's insistence a grave mistake. "Settle for what you can," they advised. "Get your foot in the door—that's the important thing. Then come back when the contract is reopened and talk about pesticides." But Chavez felt he had to hold out for the pesticide provisions as a matter of keeping faith with UFWOC's members. They did not want him to return with a contract unless it contained ironclad protections against pesticide poisonings: that is all there was to it.

In September, 1969, Chavez testified before a U.S. Senate committee, "The issue of the health and safety of farm workers in California and throughout the United States is the single most important issue facing the United Farm Workers Organizing Committee." He produced statistics which suggested that about 80 percent of farm workers experience some effects from pesticides during the year.

The antipesticide activities of UFWOC have already had an effect. The state Department of Agriculture banned the use of DDT on grapes and most other crops, as of April 1, 1970, and on all crops in California as of October 1. And when UFWOC renegotiated its contract with Perelli-Minetti in September, 1969, it succeeded in incorporating the same pesticide provisions which had deadlocked that summer's negotiations with the twelve table-grape growers. The key sections were as follows.

A. A Health and Safety Committee shall be formed consisting of equal numbers of workers' representatives . . . and P-M representatives. . . .

B. The following shall not be used: DDT, Aldrin, Dieldrin, and Endrin. Other chlorinated hydrocarbons shall not be applied without the necessary precautions.

C. The Health and Safety Committee shall recommend the proper and safe use of organic phosphates including, but not limited to parathion. The Company shall notify the Health and Safety Committee . . . before the application of organic phosphate material. . . . The Health and Safety Committee shall recommend the length of time during which farm workers will not be permitted to enter the treated field. . . .

D. If P-M uses organic phosphates, it shall pay for the expense for all farm workers applying the phosphates, of one baseline cholinesterase test and other additional tests if recommended by a doctor. The results of all said tests shall immediately be given by P-M to the . . . Committee. The Committee will also be given:
   1. A plan showing the size and location of fields and a list of the crops. . . .

2. Pesticides, insecticides, and herbicides used, including brand names plus active ingredients, registration number on the label, and manufacturers' batch or lot numbers.

   a. Dates and times applied or to be applied.
   b. Location of crops or plants treated or to be treated.
   c. Amount of each application.
   d. Formulation.
   e. Method of application.
   f. Persons who applied the pesticide.

These provisions cut the ground from under industry spokesmen who had claimed that UFWOC's position on pesticides proved that it only wanted to "rule or ruin." Upon inspection, the union's desires with respect to pesticides proved to be nothing more or less than good preventive medicine.

In the spring of 1970, negotiations resumed between UFWOC and Lionel Steinberg, representing three of the Coachella Valley growers who had been involved in the previous summer's abortive talks. A committee of the National Conference of Catholic Bishops was instrumental in bringing the parties together again and keeping the negotiations going. The committee included Bishops Hugh Donahoe of Fresno and Joseph Donnelly of Hartford, Connecticut—both experts in labor-management relations—and Archbishop Timothy Manning of Los Angeles. The committee staff was headed by Monsignor George G. Higgins of Washington, D.C.

The Church has helped Chavez and the farm labor movement many times since Father McDonnell introduced him to *Rerum novarum* nearly twenty years ago. This latest assistance may well be the most valuable of all, and may prove the last time Chavez needs to seek help from anyone outside his immediate organizational family.

Steinberg and Chavez signed a contract on March 31, in the chancery of the Los Angeles Archdiocese. Two other Coachella Valley grape growers, Kelvin and Cecil Larsen, thereupon announced that they would sign identical contracts if their employees voted to join the union. Kelvin Larsen had been touring the country, as part of the industry's "truth squad," claiming that his workers would reject UFWOC if ever given a chance. Given the chance, they voted in favor of the union, 152 to 2. The Larsen brothers signed contracts;

the wire stories did not indicate how much crow they ate or how it was cooked.

Next, William Smeds and Sons, in Fresno County, signed—the first table-grape grower in the San Joaquin Valley to do so. Then, on May 20, came the breakthrough the Delano strikers had been pointing toward for over four and a half years. Two of the largest Delano table-grape growers, Bianco Fruit Corporation and Bruno Dispoto, signed contracts. They had been two of the very first firms struck in September, 1965, and two of the most extreme in their opposition to AWOC, FWA, and UFWOC. Their agreement to terms was thus particularly symbolic—but it was also particularly substantial. These were giants of the industry, operating more than 3,200 acres of vineyards and producing 1.2 million boxes of table grapes a year.

These contracts call for wage increases of 25 to 35 cents an hour; employer contributions to the UFWOC health and welfare fund; an additional contribution to go into an "economic development fund" to aid workers displaced due to age or mechanization; protections against pesticides; and "successor clauses" which tie the union contract to the land regardless of whether ownership is transferred.

At the time of the signing, Bruno Dispoto said, "We worked hard on this contract. It is one that we can live with, one that should interest other growers in the industry." The last clause is the key. Some 95 percent of California's table-grape production was not covered by union contract at that time.

Can the sales of union-picked grapes be encouraged as effectively as the sales of nonunion grapes were discouraged? The boxes in which fresh produce is packed are usually left in the back rooms of markets. Will consumers go to the trouble of finding out whether boxes of grapes bear UFWOC's union label of a black thunderbird on a red and white background? Or can some other means of notification be devised?—for example, bunches individually packaged in plastic bags carrying the union label.

If answers to such questions are forthcoming—if the sales of growers with contracts flourish while others continue to languish—it is difficult to see that any rational agribusinessman would choose to go on committing economic suicide. There is one important new element in the equation: UFWOC is no longer standing entirely alone against the whole table-grape industry. Dispoto, Bianco, and the other companies under contract will be promoting their own product, which will be tantamount to discouraging sales of the nonunion product.

In short, UFWOC has driven a wedge into the table-grape industry, and it will never again constitute a united front against unionization. Henceforth, one portion of the industry will, in effect, be working with the union to persuade the other portion of the industry to move from the labor practices of the late nineteenth century to those of the late twentieth. During most of the history of the farm labor movement, California growers have employed a strategy of "divide and conquer" against nascent unions. A union is now, for the first time, in a position to use the same leverage on the industry.

In the winter of 1968–69, the strain of the grueling contest with the table-grape industry aggravated an old back ailment of Chavez's. He was bedridden for months. Senator Edward Kennedy took an interest in the case, as he took a heightened interest in several of his brother's concerns after Robert Kennedy's assassination. Ted Kennedy arranged to have Dr. Janet Travell, who had successfully treated a similar condition in President John F. Kennedy, visit Delano. Dr. Travell placed Chavez on a regimen which will apparently restore him to health in time; it includes a rocking chair very similar to President Kennedy's.

For many months, Chavez was able to make only rare appearances at union meetings, and then in obvious agony. At this writing, in May, 1970, he is still in some pain. It lends poignancy to his repeated reminders to the membership that sacrifice and suffering are required to build a union.

Cesar Chavez is called "saintly," "heroic," and, more frequently than any other adjective, "charismatic." If the currently fashionable catchword, "charisma," has any valid meaning at all—and in most contexts it does not—it means that a leader holds sway over his followers by some ineffable, almost supernatural, personal quality. This is almost exactly the converse of Chavez's distinguishing characteristics. Charismatic leadership, in many opportunities to do so, has never organized the industry of agriculture. It is doubtful that strictly personal leadership can prevail over any well-entrenched institutional power. All men are mortal; charismatic leaders are men; therefore, they are mortal. Without something added by others, their charisma, and their movements, tend to die with them.

Chavez is, fundamentally, a very good, shrewd, hard-working organizer of unorganized people, equipped with an unusually well-integrated philosophy of how to go about it, and why. Even if it were true that he has "charisma," whatever that may mean, he deserves to be honored not for that but for building social structures which will go on fulfilling their functions regardless of the personal qualities of his successors. His basic method, which has amply proved its value to the farm labor movement, is potentially of equal value to many other groups trying to win for themselves a better life.

8. Maker of Men:
Cesar Chavez (Part 2)

The accomplishments of Cesar Estrada Chavez, in trade union terms alone, are enough for any man's lifetime, and enough to make his organization a fork in the farm labor trail from which there can be no turning back. Even though his hand was forced at least two years prematurely, he had built so well that FWA-UFWOC was able to negotiate the first legitimate union contract in the history of California agriculture (Schenley); win the first true representation election (Di Giorgio); win all the other elections growers were willing to allow; win all the card checks growers permitted; operate hiring halls which it had been said could never work in agriculture; negotiate, renegotiate, and enforce more than a dozen contracts, covering several thousand workers with wage classifications, health insurance, paid vacations, sick leave, unemployment insurance, grievance procedures, seniority rights, and other benefits which growers had always said agriculture could not possibly grant.

But traditional trade union gains were not the beginning of Cesar Chavez's story, and they will not be the end. Even if California agriculture were to disappear, and the entire state were converted into freeways and parking lots, many of the accomplishments of Cesar Chavez would endure. Social movements ramify. Chavez, more than anyone else, has converted the farm labor movement into an authentic movement, with myriad ramifications.

To begin with, the farm labor movement is today a more nearly full-blown movement than ever before, in that it appeals to more people, from more sections of society.

In the mid-1930's, a number of Eastern liberals made common cause with the embattled Southern Tenant Farmers Union and brought "the plight of the sharecropper" to widespread attention. A March of Time film on the subject was widely distributed; the National Share-croppers Fund was established.

In the late 1930's, a Simon J. Lubin Society was formed in California to attempt to translate into constructive programs the public sympathy and indignation aroused by John Steinbeck and others. A decade later, popular concern was again aroused by the strike of the National Farm Labor Union against the Di Giorgio Fruit Company. Another ten years went by, and there was another limited awakening, brought about by the activities of the Agricultural Workers Organizing Committee. A California Citizens Committee for Agricultural Labor was formed in 1959, an Emergency Committee to Aid Farm Workers in 1961, and Citizens for Farm Labor in 1963.

Most of these expressions of concern soon flickered out; a few still exist. Most were limited to urban intellectuals; a few were broader in their appeal. But none of them has ever compared with the breadth or depth or longevity of support inspired by Cesar Chavez and his Delano group. Without deliberately setting out to do so, he has created a movement bringing together population groups which formerly did not know one another or labored under misconceptions about one another.

Catholics who have never been in a Protestant church and never associated with Protestants in any meaningful way have worked day by day with representatives of the Migrant Ministry and found them admirable people. Atheists who have long thought of Catholic priests as authoritarian, and of Catholic laymen as barefoot and pregnant, have found them to be no more authoritarian, unshod, or pregnant than themselves.

Young liberals and radicals, accustomed to thinking of labor leaders as overstuffed and complacent, have seen Paul Schrade of the UAW, Bill Kircher of the AFL-CIO Department of Organization, and others, dedicating themselves to the Delano movement as selflessly as the hottest-eyed Berkeleyan. And moderates who have thought of student activists as wild, pot-smoking, and irresponsible have found that the student volunteers who go to Delano are sober, responsible young men and women.

Old suspicions, jealousies, and feelings of superiority or inferiority have begun to fade between Anglos, Mexicans, Filipinos, and Negroes, as they work together in the Delano movement. The old feelings have not entirely disappeared. Some of the Filipinos who gave so much to the movement feel that they have been slighted in the UFWOC structure, and that their representation on the executive committee—Larry Itliong and Philip Vera Cruz—is "tokenism." Some Anglo fruit pickers from Oklahoma and Arkansas consider UFWOC a "Meskin" union, and want no part of it. Some Mexicans and Filipinos want to keep Anglos out because they are afraid of being "taken over."

But John Gregory Dunne is far off the mark when he asserts, in *Delano,* that Cesar Chavez is "just short of pathologically suspicious of Anglos." Perhaps Chavez is suspicious of Anglo reporters who come to Delano for a day or two and then return to the city to write their stories—but that is not because they are Anglos. He has known reporters of all ethnic groups to write misleading stories.

If any criticism were justified, it would be quite the opposite from Dunne's: that Chavez has leaned overly heavily on Anglo aides who are not and never have been farm workers. These assistants have included Jim Drake, Bill Esher, Kathy Lynch, Leroy Chatfield, Wendy Goepel, David Fishlow, Peggy McGivern, Marian Moses, David Averbuck, Jerome Cohen, Fred Ross, Doug Adair, and others. This was a major departure from Chavez's original ideal of farm workers' self-sufficiency. But when FWA was thrust into the grape strike with only a few days' notice, survival required instant expertise in economic research, law, fund-raising, writing, and other technical skills which farm workers did not possess. UFWOC owes its existence to Anglos who volunteered such skills, as well as to the strikers who provided the "infantry."

As time has gone by, farm workers have gained self-assurance and sophistication. Many leaders have emerged: Julio Hernandez, Marcos Muñoz, Andy Imutan, Richard and Manuel Chavez (Cesar's brother and cousin), Lupe Murgia, Tony Orendain, Pete Velasco, Eliseo Medina, Manuel Vasquez, Hope Lopez, Mack Lyons, and scores of others.

The boycott is proving a superb training ground. At least a hundred men and women who had previously done nothing but farm work all their lives have been sent into more than thirty major cities, where they must speak before strangers, set up committees, improvise without day-to-day direction, sink or swim. They are learning to swim, and swim well. When they return to Delano from their diaspora, they will be incomparably the largest, most resourceful cadre the farm labor movement has ever had. UFWOC will need them all if growers start rushing to sign contracts, for it takes a great many competent people to negotiate union contracts and operate hiring halls.

It is doubtful that Cesar Chavez ever imagined he would become a symbol for "brown consciousness"—for *la raza* (all persons of Mexican ancestry, whether first, second, third generation or more)—but that is what he has become. Probably more than any other single figure—more than Anthony Quinn, the actor; Richard Gonzales, the tennis star; Edward Roybal or Henry Gonzalez, the politicians; Lee Treviño, the golfer; or any of the numerous boxing champions of Mexican descent—Chavez has demonstrated by his bearing and deeds that it is a source of pride to be a Chicano.

This is a notable achievement in a part of the country where the phrase "prune picker" has long been considered a gross insult, and where a Social Distance Scale developed by Professor Emory Bogardus of the University of Southern California revealed that most Anglos relegated Mexicans to a status lower than Negroes.

Organizations of the Spanish-speaking have come and gone in California. When the Delano strike began, at least four such organizations claimed to represent the Mexican and Mexican-American "community": American GI Forum, League of United Latin American Citizens (LULAC), Mexican American Political Association (MAPA), and Community Service Organization (CSO). In truth, however, there was no "community." There was often jealousy between these groups. Every new leader who emerged was suspected of selfish personal ambitions.

During the early years of FWA, the Spanish-speaking organizations ignored Chavez—even CSO, which largely owed him its existence— and he tried to ignore them. He had better things to do than become involved in organizational jockeying. When the Delano strike began in 1965, some CSO and MAPA chapters took a neutral position, and the Delano CSO chapter actually opposed the strike. But by the time of the *peregrinación* to Sacramento in the spring of 1966, it was apparent to even the most jaundiced observers that Chavez was without selfish ambitions, and that he was uniting and uplifting *la raza* as no one ever had before. Spanish-speaking groups rushed to embrace him, and to pretend that they had supported him all along.

Old rivalries began to drop away. Unifying conferences were held to work on political action, police brutality, education, and other problems of common concern—including farm labor. Chavez had always said that the place to strike an ecumenical spark, which could bring California's million and a half residents of Mexican heritage together, was among farm workers. Events proved him right.

Chavez does not worry unduly about the problems of growers: "Let them put their own house in order; my job is to help workers put theirs in order." Inadvertently, however, he bids fair to have a significant impact on the housekeeping of growers, and in the process to make an accurate prophet of Fred Van Dyke. Van Dyke maintained that growers were "too set in their ways" to modernize their production, marketing, and other management practices until the pressure of organized workers forced them to.

Grapes of the varieties grown around Delano have for years been overproduced by at least 25 percent. Grower-shippers have cut each other's throats, seeing who could get to market first, and letting the devil take the hindmost. Prices were a roller-coaster ride, with many ups and downs. Only a man with iron nerve, a lot of capital, and even more luck could prosper.

In 1966, for the first time, growers of wine and table grapes began meeting with state agricultural marketing agencies to try to bring production closer into line with demand. They would no doubt have denied that this move had anything whatever to do with the activities of Cesar Chavez. But if it is a coincidence, it is a striking one.

By surviving—not to say thriving—in the face of great adversity, Chavez and the United Farm Workers Organizing Committee have had a substantial impact on the American labor movement. Organized labor is not likely to be reconstituted by tired liberals and cynical journalists sneering, "Why aren't you more energetic and idealistic?" But organized labor may be changed, and has been changed, by the example of a fraternally affiliated union, which has to assume responsibility for its members, which has to deal with practical problems every day, yet which retains an élan, a sense of humor, a sense of anger, a sense of high adventure.

Organized labor has given UFWOC at least $600,000 since 1965. It has given perhaps as much again in legal and technical counsel, contributions in kind, lobbying assistance. Richard Groulx, head of the prestigious Alameda County Central Labor Council, and other labor leaders have gone to jail for sit-ins in support of the grape strike and boycott.

Such support is not a one-way process. UFWOC has given organized labor a great deal in return. Renewed confidence, for one thing: confidence in the justice of its mission; confidence in its ability to cope with unfavorable odds. The vigor of organized labor's recent political efforts in the face of "middle America's" swing to the right was probably inspired at least in part by UFWOC's never-say-die spirit in the face of far more conservative and tightly organized opposition. Against great odds, the AFL-CIO almost elected one of its friends to the Presidency in 1968, and did block the confirmation of one of its enemies as Supreme Court justice in 1969.

There can be little doubt that the AFL-CIO's recent interest in consumer boycotts stems from UFWOC's successful application of this technique. AFL-CIO leaders must have reasoned that if a small union could bring about a 25 percent reduction in nationwide sales of a fresh fruit not identifiable by any brand name or trademark, then comparatively large and affluent unions should, through consumer education, be able to affect the sales of products prominently bearing such labels as "General Electric."

One of the problems with which a successful social movement must deal is the problem of success itself. In some ways, Cesar Chavez probably wishes that he and his movement were not so widely known. With coverage in *Time, The New Yorker,* and many other national publications, has come a mounting number of requests for help from farm workers in other areas.

Chavez has to steel himself against these pleas for assistance which flow in from throughout California and the nation. A scant twenty or thirty miles north of Delano, for example, lies a rich citrus-growing belt, in which many workers have grievances over pesticides, wages, sanitation, and other indignities. "When are you going to send somebody up to help us?" they ask. "We're so close. Surely you could spare someone for just a little while."

At one time, Chavez felt there could be no harm in lending the UFWOC name to self-starting efforts in Florida, Wisconsin, Texas, and elsewhere. But he soon learned otherwise. Debts were incurred; political allies were confused; and, most serious, local farm workers' hopes were raised in vain. A strike which began in the Lower Rio Grande Valley of Texas in 1966 was particularly disillusioning. It was started by friends of the Delano movement who thought that their devotion to the cause could make up for all things, including the fact that they had done no preliminary organizing.

From then on, Chavez firmly rejected distractions and dilutions of effort. "You can either organize, or you can strike. You cannot do both at the same time." To friends, he confides that nothing would make him happier than to have the present strike resolved so he could get back to his first love, organizing in new areas: the face-to-face kind of organizing which introduces strangers to one another and starts them working together in an organic social structure.

The Delano movement has introduced a number of innovative techniques which have not been lost on social reformers engaged in other movements.

One of the earliest Delano innovations was a newspaper, entitled *El Malcriado,* unlike any other labor paper published in this country. The title is ironic, idiomatic, virtually untranslatable. It means "the ill-bred" or "lowly born," but the implication is something to this effect: "They may look down on us, but we shall inherit the earth, and along the way we'll have a lot more fun than they will."

From its first issue, *El Malcriado* was a saucy, free-swinging affair, in which news and editorials were often indistinguishable, and generously spiced with cartoons, invective, and jokes, sometimes verging on the slanderous. Indeed, the paper was forced to suspend publication for a time because of libel suits. The style is not Chavez's own, but he asks only, "Are there people willing to do the work of putting it out?" (There are.) And, more importantly, "Do the members like it?" (They do.)

Even more highly original was El Teatro Campesino, or Farm Workers Theater. In this combination of commedia del arte and Brecht, farm workers themselves became actors, entertainers, and instructors of their fellow workers through sketches in which the stock parts, rather than Harlequin and Columbine, were broadly caricatured growers, labor contractors, strikers, strikebreakers, and politicians.

El Teatro Campesino is equally effective at the side of a struck field, and in a university community, raising funds.

Of all Chavez's innovations, however, the most fundamental is his attempt to build a union which is not just a vending machine—not like the unions which increasingly resemble the businesses they meet across the bargaining table. Chavez has always envisioned a union which is a meaningful community of human beings, with contributions to make in many other sectors besides the economic. This vision is taking tangible form in Delano. On forty acres of land on the west side of town, previously unused because of its high alkaline content, a UFWOC community is rising.

A cooperative gas station is already in operation. There is a clinic. Chavez's first attempt at a community institution, the credit union, is still functioning, and his wife, Helen, is still its unpaid manager. A community center is nearing completion, to provide facilities for recreation, evening classes, and the like.

This development is further advanced in Delano than anywhere else, but Chavez intends that eventually a network of such community centers will spread throughout rural California, and beyond California, wherever there is a UFWOC local. It is part of the vision of Cesar Chavez that the good life does not require a move to a great city. He has seen how big cities estrange men from nature and from themselves. He is trying to make it possible for men to remain on the land in dignity. In so doing, he has set his course against a worldwide urbanward tendency. This is one of the respects in which it is not putting the case too strongly to say that the Delano movement has revolutionary implications—if it be understood that the profoundest revolutions do not involve shot and shell.

How "radical" is Cesar Chavez? Tremendously. Not very. Everything depends on one's point of view, and one's terms.

If "radical" means "getting to the root," if it means facing realities unflinchingly and without cant, then Chavez is a genuine radical. He has grasped firmly many nettles which previous incarnations of the farm labor movement overlooked or avoided. As between organizing workers and intermediaries, Chavez has organized only workers. As between organizing workers who are marginally attached to agriculture and those who are committed to it, he has organized only the latter.

The farm labor trail has divided, historically, over the question, "What shall we settle for?" Worker organizations have often settled for wage increases, and growers have often been willing to grant them, knowing that by the next season the organizing drive would have disappeared. Chavez has shown that an organization which can be purchased so easily is not a proper union. He and UFWOC settle for nothing less than lasting, codified acknowledgment of their existence.

Where the trail forks between the lowest common denominator and one high enough to represent faithfully the feelings of his membership, Chavez has always chosen the higher denominator, even though it has on a number of occasions cost him some fair-weather friends and added to the number of his enemies (or adversaries, as he prefers to call them). Although he is no believer in the "class struggle" or other Marxian formulas, he does not shrink from drawing the line between group interests when his own union's experience suggests a line must be drawn. He has little patience with those who try to play both sides of the field in the Delano strike. His enemies (or adversaries) cry that he has "split the community" and that "Delano was such a happy place before." Others lament that he has "divided the Catholic Church."

Chavez points out that "division" was there all the time; people in privileged positions merely could not see it—or did not want to. He has brought it into the open, and forced people to deal with it, one way or the other. "Sorry, but you can't have it both ways. Either you're for continuing injustice or you're for justice and you do something about it. If you do something about it, you're bound to make somebody unhappy. The more they have benefited from injustice, the unhappier they are going to be." As for "splitting the Catholic Church," some growers may have reduced their contributions and bequests, but most communicants are probably proud that someone of their faith is demonstrating that it is not necessary to be an atheist or agnostic in order to be an effective social reformer.

A successful farm labor union will by its very nature "subvert" the present rural California social order under which elected representatives and administrators have served the minority who own the land rather than the majority who work on it; under which justice is not blind, but peeks out from under her handkerchief to see if a plaintiff or defendant has brown skin and calluses on his hands; under which schools, newspapers, police departments, churches, and every other social institution covertly or overtly perpetuates the premise that landowners are a class above, landworkers a class below.

If it be revolutionary to change such a social order to one which is more democratic, then farm labor unionism is revolutionary. But in the usual, pejorative sense of the word, Chavez, and farm workers generally, are not "radical" at all. Under the circumstances, it is surprising that the exceptions to this rule are so rare. Farm laborers believe in the American dream better than almost anyone else in the country: better than stunned ghetto-dwellers, stoned drop-outs, drifting suburbanites; better than growers who wrap themselves in the flag.

To allege, as some do, that Chavez is "out to destroy California agriculture" is preposterous. He is the least vindictive of men. Of all farm labor leaders, he best understands agriculture and its real problems as distinguished from its fantasies. He well realizes that the interests of the union's members presuppose a healthy agricultural industry. When growers of grapes or any other major commodity recognize the union, Chavez plans to turn his nationwide apparatus around, and have his community coordinators urge consumers to buy more grapes, or whatever crop is involved.

Chavez does not want to cripple or destroy California agriculture; but California agriculture wants to cripple or destroy Chavez. If growers succeed in doing so, it will not be the first Pyrrhic victory in the annals of countermovements, but there will have been none more Pyrrhic. They will not have killed the movement. They will only have killed their chances of dealing with a man as honorable as Chavez.

The desires of farm workers are essentially conservative, in that they include only those things which the American economy has demonstrated it is quite capable of conferring upon other workers: reasonable wages, reasonable safety and other working conditions, reasonable fringe benefits, reasonable job security, and underlying all a reasonable voice in determining what is reasonable. The present-day California farm labor movement does not call for the breaking up of great estates and redistribution of the land. It calls only for enforcement of the "160-acre limitation" which is already on the statute books. UFWOC has recently filed a suit toward that end.

Despite many disappointments, Chavez, other UFWOC leaders, and the membership retain a basic confidence in the democratic process. True, they are wary of administrative agencies. This attitude hurts the feelings of some persons from within those agencies, who consider themselves friends of the movement. The union's wariness is not directed against individuals; it is directed against bureaucracies in which individuals, however sympathetic, are not free agents. As Chavez once put it, "You can't build an organization around something that can be given or taken away at the whim of some bureau chief. We have to build around programs we can be sure of—and the only programs we can be absolutely sure of are those where we do the policing ourselves."

But for all this caution, Chavez depends in many ways upon the ultimate workability of representative democracy, with an executive branch and an independent judiciary. Although the union has seldom if ever won a case in a municipal or county court, it keeps trying, and often wins on appeal. The union's confidence in the integrity of the higher levels of the judiciary is reinforced by the experience of California Rural Legal Assistance, an agency which came into existence a few months after the Delano strike began. CRLA has repeatedly demonstrated that growers, county boards of supervisors, welfare departments, and the Governor himself can be challenged in the courts, successfully. Every year, these persons try to strike back at CRLA through its funding agency, the Office of Economic Opportunity, but to date CRLA's grant has been renewed on each occasion.

Ideally, Chavez might prefer a situation in which the balance of power between the union and the growers was so close that neither would need to rely on intervention by government mediators, OEO-funded agencies, or any other third party. Realistically, however, he knows that the union is not likely to achieve such a situation without the protection of a state or national labor relations act which requires the holding of representation elections when a union can demonstrate that a certain percentage of the workers want it (the figure is 30 percent in other industries), and which requires the employer to bargain in good faith if one union or another wins a majority.

Chavez therefore supports collective bargaining bills sponsored in the U.S. Senate by Senators Harrison Williams, Eugene McCarthy,

George McGovern, Jacob Javits, Edward Kennedy, William Proxmire, and ten others; and in the House of Representatives by Congressmen James O'Hara, Phillip Burton, Jeffery Cohelan, and fifty-two others.

Growers are pressing for their own version of farm labor legislation, sponsored by their tireless friend, Senator George Murphy. This bill appears at first glance to provide for orderly negotiation but would, in practice, severely hobble farm unionism. Chavez has countered by asking for legislation which would exempt agricultural workers from those sections of the Taft-Hartley and Landrum-Griffin Acts defining secondary boycotts and recognition picketing as "unfair labor practices."

Some of Chavez's friends were taken aback by this demand, since the movement had for years marched under the slogan of "Equal rights for farm workers." Then Chavez explained: he was asking for the same rights other workers had enjoyed *when they were at a comparable stage in their organization.*

The Wagner Act of 1935 was openly "pro-union," in order more nearly to equalize the bargaining strengths of workers and employers. The Wagner Act permitted secondary boycotts: that is, boycotts against businesses which were not directly involved in a labor dispute but which handled struck goods. The Wagner Act also permitted organizational picketing: that is, picketing before a union had been recognized as collective bargaining agent, in order to pressure a company into holding a representation election. By 1947, most industries had become organized, and many unions had become very powerful. Seeking a new balance of power, the Taft-Hartley Act banned some of the unions' weapons. The Landrum-Griffin Act of 1959 banned others.

Chavez says, "We too need our decent period of time to grow strong under the life-giving sun of a public policy which affirmatively favors the growth of farm unionism." He asks for a Wagner Act in agriculture, with one difference: "It should be made an unfair labor practice for a grower to employ anyone during a strike or lockout who has not actually established a permanent residence in the United States." The United Automobile Workers, and other great industrial unions, never had to contend with anything resembling California agriculture's importation of green carders. If they had, they would probably not exist today and the country's basic industries would still be wracked with labor strife.

Every social movement is, in some respects, a conspiracy against the status quo. The status quo is, in some respects, a conspiracy against every social movement. Since the status quo almost always has the greater resources, the odds are almost always against the survival of any given movement. The mortality rate is extraordinarily high. The Delano movement has survived longer than most, and seems likely to continue to survive. Why? How? We have already noted that Chavez's organizing methods were unusually thorough. But we have also noted that he was precipitated into a strike a full two years before he estimates that he would have been ready. It might be noted, too, that Chavez's organizing methods were practically identical to those used by Father McCullough's AWA in 1958–59, and by AWOC during its volunteer period of July-December, 1961, neither of which survived. What made the difference?

The "times" helped. The Delano movement benefited from America's discovery of poverty in the early 1960's, from the *aggiornamento,* or refreshening, of Catholicism under Pope John XXIII, from the civil rights movement, the student movement, the peace movement, and, most recently, from the ecology movement.

But ripe times do not, by themselves, make movements, much less sustain them through the crises and countermovements which any effective social movement is bound to generate. One keeps coming back, again and again, to Cesar Chavez.

How to account for it? Everything about the man is low-key. He is slightly below the middle height. His handshake is diffident. His smile is shy. He issues no crisp orders, but says, "What would you think if we tried such-and-such?"

He enters a public meeting so unobtrusively that one is hardly aware of his presence until he is introduced to speak. He never raises his voice in public utterances, any more than private. He brushes a persistent shock of hair from his forehead, and talks conversationally whether the gathering is large or small, broadcast, televised, or unrecorded. He makes little jokes as he goes along, but unless one is familiar with the farm workers' universe of discourse, one may not realize they are jokes, for they are invariably understated.

Then everyone holds hands with those to his right and left, and sings "Nosotros Venceremos" (We Shall Overcome). Suddenly it is over. Chavez has slipped out the back door, to another meeting, or to return to bed to rest his back. A woman who has never attended a UFWOC meeting before says, "I have just seen a great man." She has tears in her eyes. A man who has been to dozens of these meetings says, "I would trust him better than my own father. Better than my own brother. I would trust him with my life."

How to account for it?

One of the qualities which Chavez brings to his leadership—which Blackie Ford, Pat Chambers, Ernesto Galarza, Hank Hasiwar, Father McCullough, Clive Knowles, Norman Smith, and others did not—is that he is nothing but a farm laborer and farm labor organizer. He has no other profession to fall back on, as the others did. He will stay with the job until it is finished, or until it finishes him.

Some other farm labor leaders have talked of their great "dedication," and the more they talked of it, the less convincing they became. Chavez does not mention it—and the less he talks of it, the more convincing he becomes. Grape strikers have far better grounds for trusting him. He receives just $5 a week for all his personal expenses, as they do. They have seen him at close range, in small meetings, over the years, in the small day-to-day ways which make up an authentic life. They know, as certainly as it is given any man to know anything, that he will never betray them.

Another respect in which Chavez differs from some of those who preceded him is that, for all his flexibility in daily tactics, he knows where he is going and how to get there. This is a difficult quality to maintain in any social movement, but a most important one. If a reformer does not have an organizing plan he is completely sure of, he will be buffeted about by the storms which all social movements arouse, he is apt to grow hesitant or do something rash, and his followers may panic. Chavez possesses an air of calm confidence, and he communicates this quality to those around him.

Or perhaps the mystery is to be accounted for in terms of the growth which members of the Delano movement have felt in their own lives. The litmus test of a social movement is not how many members it has, how much publicity it attracts, but whether it actually changes the content of people's lives. By this test, the accomplishments of UFWOC, no matter what happens in the future, are ineffaceable.

In the traditional culture of Mexico, women's place is in *la casa*. The traditional culture is bent when Mexican families emigrate to rural California, where women must usually work in the fields to augment the family income. But, publicly at least, it is very much a man's world. Women do not venture economic or political opinions; they would not presume to speak on behalf of their husbands; they would not dare to walk a picket line.

Cesar Chavez has been a liberator in this respect. When the strike began, Dolores Huerta was made director of picketing. No one was more successful than she in persuading workers to leave the vineyards. Other women began to grow more vocal and to assume positions outside the strike kitchen.

The involvement of women in strike activity was good not only for them but for their husbands as well. One of the root purposes of the strike, after all, was to make it possible for male breadwinners to support their families in decency. In addition to everything else which may be said about it, the low-wage tradition in agriculture is profoundly destructive to a man's morale: it tells him constantly that he is incapable of supporting his family by his own efforts—that he has to be subsidized by his own wife and children.

In an even more basic way, the Delano movement may be thought of as an exercise in culture change. It is a challenge to the feudalistic, fatalistic patrón tradition of Mexico: a tradition which forces feelings of childishness and helplessness upon adults and makes them totally dependent upon the good will of the "boss." From the very beginning of FWA, Chavez said to the small groups which gathered together in house meetings, "We are not helpless. We are not pawns. If we get together, and stick together, we can change things. We can make a difference."

Cultural heritages are difficult to overcome. It is possible that Chavez himself may be perceived as a new kind of patrón. He is sensitive to this danger. He does not encourage the cries of "Viva Cesar Chavez!" which punctuate UFWOC rallies. He ducks his head, waits for the cheering to fade, and hurries on with the business of undermining the patrón tradition by building an effective, democratic organization.

At one time, in 1966, he became so troubled by the adulation—by the journalists clustering about as though he alone were the fount of all farm labor wisdom—that he turned to Father McCullough for advice. "I don't want to be an indispensable man. I want to be able to leave and know that the union will go on."

The priest reminded him, "You have told the members that they would have to sacrifice greatly. Maybe that's what you are now being called on to do: to sacrifice your privacy, to do things you feel very uncomfortable doing, for the good of the group. Maybe in a couple of years, you can step out of the spotlight. But right now this is just something you have to accept—a cross you have to bear."

Chavez took Father McCullough's advice. He does what he must do for the sake of the organization, but he looks forward to the day when he can "go to the mountains or some place where it's quiet, and read all the classics in Spanish and English . . ."

Of all the ways Cesar Chavez has changed the content of men's lives, none is more fundamental, none more daring, and none will be remembered longer than the covenant with nonviolence which he himself has made, and which he asks all UFWOC members to make.

When the Delano strike began, and Chavez obtained from both AWOC and FWA members a pledge that it would be conducted nonviolently, his beliefs were probably largely pragmatic. Violence would be counterproductive; damaging growers' property would only stiffen their resistance; assaulting strikebreakers would only alienate church and liberal sympathy and support. And, as Congressman Phillip Burton recently said, "Nonviolence is the greatest selling point we have in Washington. I know all about the Watts business, and the squeaking wheel getting the grease, and all of that. But this is different. If the union ever starts using strong-arm tactics, we're dead. You can forget about any farm labor legislation. . . ."

The UFWOC discipline apparently did not forbid verbal violence, and there seems to have been a good deal of it. And sometimes the ban on physical violence wavered. A few pickets peppered strikebreakers with marbles. A few growers' tires were flattened. A few windows in strikebreakers' homes were broken. But, by and large, the discipline was well maintained—astonishingly well maintained under the particular circumstances.

There was nothing in the cultural backgrounds of Mexican and Filipino strikers to prepare them for the theory and practice of nonviolence. Quite the contrary. There are strong strains in both cultures which not only accept violence as inevitable, but glorify it as one of the surest proofs that one is *muy macho*—very much a man. The same strain is not unknown in the culture of the United States.

What is more, growers and their allies engaged in a great deal of provocation, obviously designed to goad the strikers into retaliating. Reliable eyewitness accounts, and photographs, document many instances of growers, supervisory personnel, and armed guards stepping on pickets' toes, punching and elbowing them, shooting holes in their picket signs, driving cars at them. One picket was run over and nearly killed. On at least four occasions, arsonists tried to burn the union headquarters. A union bus was damaged by fire. The cooperative gas station was bombed twice. A cross at the Forty Acres was desecrated.

As time went by, Chavez's lieutenants reported that it was becoming increasingly difficult to maintain nonviolent discipline among the rank and file. Chavez's answer was to undertake a long fast during the Lenten season of 1968, to rededicate himself to the principle of active but peaceable resistance, to do penance for the occasions when he may have given way to feelings of hatred—and, although this was never publicly stated, to do penance for the wavering faith of some of his followers.

Amid the sixteen- and eighteen-hour days which Chavez has devoted to the strike and boycott, he has somehow found time to study philosophy. He has moved toward ever deeper convictions about nonviolence, on a number of levels: pragmatic, psychological, moral. At a meeting of several hundred union members and friends in February, 1969, Chavez rose from a sickbed to say:

"It is for God, not us, to know what is going to be the eventual outcome of what we are doing. All we can be sure of is what we are doing right now, today. There is no such thing as means and ends. Everything that we do is an end, in itself, that we can never erase. That is why we must make all our actions the kind we would like to be judged on, as though they might be our last—which they might well be, who knows? That is why we will not let ourselves be provoked by our adversaries into behaving hatefully. . . ."

This kind of education—which might seem more appropriate in a course on Existentialist Ethics than in a meeting of farm laborers, most of whom have not completed elementary school—is Chavez's last and greatest effort at changing people's lives by changing their culturally inherited ways of looking at themselves and the world.

He is challenging the long-standing, deeply embedded folkways which equate aggressiveness with manliness in the cultures of Mexico, the Philippines, the United States—and in the culture of labor organizing itself. It is a breathtaking challenge. Up to this point, at least, the power of Chavez's example is winning the improbable gamble, and evolving some of the aspects of a new culture.

Chavez's fast in the spring of 1968 continued for twenty-five days. It nearly killed him, but it saved the union. Mutterings of "Let's give them a taste of their own medicine" are no longer heard. All the growers' recent efforts to prove sabotage by the union—and their efforts are ceaseless—have rebounded against them.

Chavez's long fast ended on March 10, with symbolic breaking of bread at an outdoor convocation attended by an estimated six thousand agricultural workers. Martin Luther King, Jr., sent a telegram which read:

> I am deeply moved by your courage in fasting as your personal sacrifice for justice through nonviolence. Your past and present commitment is eloquent testimony to the constructive power of nonviolent action and the destructive impotence of violent reprisal. You stand today as a living example of the Gandhian tradition. . . . My colleagues and I commend you for your bravery, salute you for your indefatigable work against poverty and injustice, and pray for your health and continuing service as one of the outstanding men of America. The plight of your people and ours is so grave that we all desperately need the inspiring example and effective leadership you have given.

Robert Kennedy interrupted his campaign for the presidential nomination to join Chavez at the bread-breaking ceremony. Chavez was too weak to stand or speak, but a statement which he had prepared was read on his behalf.

. . . we have something the rich do not own. We have our own bodies and spirits and the justice of our cause as our weapons.

When we are really honest with ourselves we must admit that our lives are all that really belong to us. So, it is how we use our lives that determines the kind of men we are. It is my deepest belief that only by giving our lives do we find life. I am convinced that the truest act of courage, the strongest act of manliness, is to sacrifice ourselves for others in a totally nonviolent struggle for justice.

To be a man is to suffer for others. God help us to be men!

In the course of this fast, Chavez said, "La huelga is not worth the blood of a single farm worker or his child, or a single grower or his child": a more compassionate statement than any farm labor leader had made before, and an indication of the spiritual development of Chavez himself, and of his movement.

Less than a month later, Martin Luther King, Jr., was killed while helping another group of unorganized workers build a union. In less than three months, Robert Kennedy was killed, moments after his California primary victory speech in which he singled out Cesar Chavez and Dolores Huerta for special praise. The Kennedy family chose Chavez as one of twelve honorary pallbearers, in recognition of the Senator's feeling for the farm labor movement, and his friendship with Chavez.

Since the death of King, Chavez is probably America's leading practitioner of nonviolent direct action in the resolution of social problems where channels of communication and mediation are blocked or do not exist. Indeed, with Danilo Dolci and Vinoba Bhave, he is one of the great nonviolent reformers of the world. Some observers anticipate that if he continues to develop his ideas about social change, and applies them as he has done to date, Chavez will in time be considered for the Nobel Peace Prize.

Others anticipate that Cesar Chavez himself may be martyred, like his friends Kennedy and King. If the thought has crossed his mind, he does not speak of it, and it does not affect him in the slightest. He seems fully prepared to accept whatever may come his way in the quest for social justice.

". . . it is how we use our lives that determines what kind of men we are." Cesar Chavez might have added that it also determines the kind of influence we shall have. This, perhaps, brings us close to the heart of the mystery. Chavez possesses the power of a life well spent. The power of such a life lies in the fact that other men would like to spend their lives to good account, too. They are hungry for models to show the way. There are not very many to be found in this society at this time. Cesar Chavez is one of the few.

So, persons of varying backgrounds and persuasions have pledged themselves to the farm labor movement. Some renounce remunerative professional careers to donate their skills to the movement. Others, shy and inexperienced farm workers, renounce their own shyness and inexperience, and by an act of will go forth as apostles to the great Eastern cities, organizing labor-church-liberal coalitions, raising funds, debating Madison Avenue mercenaries.

To be able to say, "I am doing something worthwhile with my life; I am rising above myself; I am functioning as a real man," is the most validating thing anyone can ever say to himself. It is the source of strength of all religious movements; it is the wellspring of strength of the Delano movement.

Opponents of the farm labor movement cannot comprehend this form of power. What they cannot comprehend, they cannot combat effectively. They call Chavez a "Communist," a "dues-collector." The more they rage, the more irrelevant they become.

The union grows, and seems likely to continue growing no matter what happens to Chavez, for in the course of becoming a man himself, Cesar Chavez has been a maker of men.

Afterword

Events are moving so swiftly that it would be foolhardy to attempt to predict the future of the farm labor movement in any detail or according to any precise timetable—particularly in view of UFWOC's fondness for innovation. Certain broad tendencies may be anticipated, however.

The proximity of Mexico will continue to pose a problem for the movement. In Mexico, the United States is often referred to as the Colossus of the North. So far as the California farm labor movement is concerned, Mexico is the Colossus of the South, which, however unintentionally, has kept a long dream deferred simply by being where it is and being what it is. A poor nation, adjoining a rich nation, with a relatively open border, will always pose problems for persons at the bottom of the socio-economic heap in the rich nation. In principle, there are three solutions: to seal the border; to lower the standards of the rich nation; or to raise the standards of the poor nation. The first is undesirable; the second is unfeasible; the third is a course which should be promoted seriously by everyone who considers himself a friend of the farm labor movement. Whether the latter course will actually be pursued is another matter.

The trend toward corporation agriculture will almost certainly go on. The trend may be slowed somewhat by restrictions on "tax-loss" farming and ceilings on subsidies, but many pressures toward consolidation will continue. Unionization, contrary to some opinions, is not among these pressures. To be sure, the logistic problems of the movement would be greatly simplified if there were only a few very large growers to bargain with. Most of the leaders and members of the movement, however, actively support public policies such as the 160-acre limitation. They would prefer to deal with legitimate farmers who know what it is like to put in a hard day's work in the field.

Agriculture need not be operated by huge corporations in order to enjoy the advantages of mechanization and economies of scale. The same advantages would follow if small and medium-size growers were to share machinery cooperatively, purchase fertilizer and other supplies cooperatively, sell cooperatively—and employ labor cooperatively through a clearinghouse jointly operated by employers and employees. But most small growers will in all likelihood hold out against organization of themselves, and organization of workers, until the bitter end. And so they will go the way of other natural species and social forms which could not or would not adapt to changed circumstances.

It is no coincidence that all of UFWOC's contracts at this writing are with relatively large operators. Corporations with professional managers are less likely to function on the basis of ideology and more likely to adapt to the fact that the era of a semicaptive farm labor force is in its twilight.

As agriculture becomes ever larger in scale, it will become ever more highly mechanized. This does not mean, however, that farm labor, and the farm labor movement, will become obsolete. Some types of harvests—table grapes are a good example—require such multiple judgments of color, size, shape, and other variables that it is difficult to see how human beings can be replaced. And, in any case, agricultural machinery does not operate by itself. The change in the farm labor force will be more in types of workers needed than in numbers. The harvesting of cannery tomatoes, for instance, used to be a singularly primitive job, suited only to men with very strong backs. With the end of the bracero system, University of California technicians developed a new strain of tomatoes, and a machine to pick them. Tens of thousands of workers are still needed to sort the tomatoes as they pass along conveyor belts in the fields, but it is physically undemanding work, performed almost entirely by women.

More areas of California will be brought into production through great new irrigation projects. Agriculture will become more highly diversified. There will continue to be some seasonality in labor requirements. But farm labor needs will no longer be filled by ragged migrants and hungry foreigners. The agricultural producers who survive the 1970's will have survived, in large measure, because they have learned that it is in their own interests to have a labor force which is stable, skilled, satisfied, and solvent.

Workers and jobs will be brought together in a rational fashion, with growers knowing in advance of the season where their labor force will come from, and workers knowing in advance where their jobs will come from. Something close to year-round agricultural employment will be afforded in most parts of California. To the extent that there is "migrancy," it will resemble that of operating engineers or construction workers, rather than that of the Joads.

When there is no work, agricultural laborers will be eligible for unemployment insurance on the same basis as anyone else. All other forms of social and labor legislation will be extended to agriculture, and will be enforced as they are in other industries.

Producers of perishable crops will usually grow for a known market at a known price, under contracts signed in advance of the season, which permit management to make a fair return on its investment, and workers to receive a fair wage. It would not be unseemly for food prices to rise, if that were necessary for farm workers and owners to receive economic justice. Agricultural workers (and, to an extent, producers) have for many years been subsidizing American consumers. The price of food has risen less than other costs and disposable income, with the result that America today spends a smaller proportion of income on food than ever before—about 18 percent—and a smaller proportion of that goes to farmers (less than 40 percent) and a larger proportion to middlemen than ever before.

The farmers' and farm workers' share will increase somewhat, when agriculture begins to compete more actively for the consumers' dollar, against physicians, landlords, professional athletes, automobile manufacturers, and purveyors of other goods and services not one of which is so crucial to human existence as food. There will be some sound and fury from those who think it to their advantage to keep the national economic pie divided just as it is now. But when the sound and fury are done, it will be found that no one suffers serious dislocation as growers and farm workers begin to receive a fairer share of the national income. Rather, merchants and manufacturers and money lenders and everyone else will benefit when farm workers have a level of purchasing power comparable to that of other workers, and when agricultural producers enjoy a rate of return on investment comparable to that of other producers.

⋊   To mention a few representative examples, field workers receive less than one-third of a cent per pound for wrenching the tops off dry onions and putting the onions into "stubs" or sacks; about half a cent per pound for picking oranges; one cent a bunch for pulling and tieing carrots; about a cent a pound for cutting and field-packing broccoli. These products sell for about 20 cents to 40 cents a unit in the retail market. Wages account for as little as 1½ percent of the retail price; at most, about 5 percent. A 100 percent increase in farm workers' wages need result in no more than a 3 percent increase in the cost of food, or about one-half of one percent in the average American family's total cost of living. If the return to growers increased by a comparable amount, the total cost would still be something less than one-tenth the cost of the war in Indochina.

It may even be found that economies of mechanization, elimination of labor contractors' commissions, and other long overdue management improvements actually yield lower food prices following unionization.

There will be an agricultural workers' union. At the moment, one cannot be altogether sure what kind of a union. It could conceivably be the Teamsters, although they would have to rid themselves of their "sweetheart contract" reputation before becoming acceptable to most farm workers. There could be some union not yet discernible on the horizon.

But it looks, at this writing, as though the future belongs to Cesar Chavez and the United Farm Workers Organizing Committee. They have created fissures in the dam of grower resistance which cannot be sealed again. It even looks as though UFWOC, despite what the pundits have long said, may be able to organize California agriculture without the benefit of collective bargaining laws. Such legislation may be passed only after unionization is an accomplished and accepted fact.

If there is one great peril, perhaps, it is that the union may become the victim of its own success: that it will be overwhelmed by the demand for contracts as the dam gives way. If UFWOC does not overextend itself, and does not grow overconfident, it could within the foreseeable future have California agriculture thoroughly organized by essentially the same methods used in grapes. Citrus fruits, for example, might be next. Most growers of oranges, lemons, and grapefruit belong to Sunkist or a handful of other associations. After the union had an organizational base among the workers, the associations might be given the opportunity to conduct representation elections. If they refused, a boycott could be mounted. UFWOC has already clearly demonstrated what a nationwide consumer boycott of a particular fresh fruit can do.

Some predict that most growers will hold firm against UFWOC in the hope that the Murphy Bill, which prohibits agricultural strikes and boycotts, will become law. It would appear a singularly slender hope. In the first place, Senator Murphy does not have the votes, any more than he had them when he tried unsuccessfully to kill CRLA (California Rural Legal Assistance) in 1969. And even if there were a radically conservative reorganization of the Senate after the 1970 elections, and agricultural boycotts were outlawed, it would not halt the peregrinación of the farm labor movement. Chavez and his followers, and friends throughout the country, are prepared to go to jail if necessary rather than submit to repressive and discriminatory legislation. The spirit of the age has passed the agricultural dinosaurs by. Any attempt now to stifle farm workers' unionization by legislative, administrative, or judicial decree would have an opposite effect from that intended: it would unleash boycotts and protests beyond anything seen before.

As California agriculture goes, so goes the agriculture of much of the rest of the nation. Many of California's farming corporations and conglomerates also operate in Arizona, Texas, Michigan, and other states. They may all be organized in the proximate future. Agricultural patterns differ; a farm workers' union will need to be flexible and pluralistic to deal with the small fruit growers of the Hood River Valley of Oregon, the Yakima Valley of Washington, and the many other local and regional variations in ownership and land usage.

But there will be a union. Even if all the present leaders of the movement were to falter and all its present friends were to drop away, other leaders and other friends would spring up, like warriors from dragon's teeth. The movement will go on, because of the nature of the seeds which have been sown, and the nature of the soil in which they lie.

The planting began long ago. The grains were small, and people thought that somehow made it all right: small grains of bondage, out of sight and out of mind. Indians, Chinese, Japanese, Hindus, Filipinos, Dust Bowl refugees, migrants, bindle stiffs, prisoners of war, children, convicts, wetbacks, braceros, green carders: they passed in ghostly review, and we closed our eyes and asked no questions as long as fruits and vegetables reached us bountifully and cheaply.

As ye sow, so shall ye reap. The seeds of bondage produced alien strains which choked other plantings in our fields. Along with its lush fruits and vegetables, the California harvest yielded human debasement, and the estrangement of man from his work, from the land, from his fellow man.

This bitter harvest will not continue much longer. The tares will be rooted out, and sweeter harvests will begin, because the soil of America is, in the last analysis, congenial to the seeds of the farm labor movement, and uncongenial to injustice.

Americans are sometimes tolerant of unfairness for long periods of time. They are capable of selfishness, prejudice, and other human failings. But the value system of the United States stresses the very qualities called for by the farm labor movement: freedom of association, self-determination, fair play. It is always to the advantage of any social movement if, rather than demanding a whole new set of social values, it asks society simply to live up to those which it already professes.

And even when Americans are relatively unmoved by abstract moral appeals, they may often be touched by a single story, or picture, which depicts a living instance of injustice. Americans tend to be sentimental, sympathetic to underdogs. They do not care for contests in which a great preponderance of power is on one side. When Senator Robert Kennedy said, with almost his last breath, "This is a great, an unselfish, a compassionate country," he had particular reference to the farm labor movement and its prospects.

There will be a farm workers' union, too, because the movement has a workable program at last. H. L. Mitchell, elder statesman of the movement in length of service, once said, "Sure, you can organize farm workers. The problem is, how do you keep them organized?" A quiet, gentle, confident, determined man from Delano appears to have found answers to that question.

But in the end, the primary engine of the movement will not be other people's sense of fair play, nor one particular strategy or structure as against another; it will be nothing so much as farm workers' own basic insistence upon justice, no matter what ugly names they may be called, no matter what legal obstacles may be thrown across the trail, no matter how many paydays they may have to sacrifice.

There will be a farm labor union because farm workers demand it, as part of the larger wind which is rising and the rivers which are flowing among all manner of disinherited peoples in the United States and throughout the world.

Suggested Readings

Many of the most useful materials on the farm labor movement are unavailable through commercial channels. The hearings of the La Follette Committee, referred to in Chapter 2, are long out of print, but might be found in a good university library. The full citation is United States Senate Committee on Education and Labor, *Hearings on Violations of Free Speech and Rights of Labor, Pursuant to S. Res. 266, 74th Congress.*

Labor Unionism in American Agriculture, by Stuart M. Jamieson, a scholarly history of the movement up to 1941, was never published commercially, only as a government document: U.S. Bureau of Labor Statistics Bulletin No. 836, 1945. If one has a good relationship with a congressman or senator, one may still be able to obtain a copy.

The United States Census of Agriculture is valuable in many ways if one is able to read between the innumerable lines of raw data on size and ownership of farms, use of hired labor, and so forth. It is conducted every five years, and is obtainable from the Superintendent of Documents, U.S. Government Printing Office, Washington, D.C. The most recent Census of Agriculture comes in some fifty volumes, at prices ranging from 40 cents to $5.00 per volume. California, Volume I, Part 48, is $3.50.

Master's theses and doctoral dissertations have been written on the Southern Tenant Farmers Union, the strawberry and sugar workers' strike discussed in Chapter VI, and many other aspects of the farm labor movement, but would be available only if one has interlibrary loan privileges. The same is true of Fred Van Dyke's writings and more than thirty Agricultural Workers Organizing Committee research papers, which are stored in the Bancroft Library, University of California, Berkeley.

Information about Ernesto Galarza's *Strangers in Our Fields, Merchants of Labor,* and *Spiders in the House* may be obtained by writing to Dr. Galarza, 1031 Franquette Ave., San Jose, California. Information about Henry Anderson's *Fields of Bondage* and *A Harvest of Loneliness* is obtainable from Mr. Anderson, P. O. Box 1173, Berkeley, California.

An American Exodus, by Paul Taylor, is a touching chronicle of the Dust Bowl refugees of the 1930's, told principally in their own words, with exemplary photographs by Dr. Taylor's wife, Dorothea Lange. Originally published in the Depression, it was reissued in 1969 by Yale University Press, both in cloth and paperback.

In Dubious Battle, John Steinbeck's version of a Communist-led strike, is deservedly less well known than *The Grapes of Wrath,* both as literature and as an interpretation of fact. Carey McWilliams' *Ill Fares the Land,* on the other hand, is undeservedly less well known than *Factories in the Field.*

As You Sow, by Walter R. Goldschmidt (New York: Harcourt, Brace, 1947) is a study of the sociological differences between a community in an area of small farms, and one in an area of corporation farms. It still repays reading—and it suggested the title of the present book.

The Harvest Labor Market in California, by Lloyd H. Fisher (Cambridge, Mass.: Harvard University Press, 1953) is especially valuable for its information on the period, around the turn of the century, when Japanese were trying, in their own way, to organize the industry.

Since the Delano strike began in 1965, the farm labor movement has been discovered by any number of journalists. Perhaps the most perceptive of the exercises in "personal journalism" to date has been Peter Matthiesen's *Sal Si Puedes* (New York: Random House, 1970).

For what it proposes to do—which is unashamedly to give UFWOC's side of every story—there is nothing to compare with *El Malcriado,* Box 130, Delano, California. The other side may be found in the *California Farm Bureau Monthly,* 2855 Telegraph Avenue, Berkeley, California.

Mitchell Slobodek's *A Selective Bibliography of California Labor History,* published in 1964, contains over twenty pages of references on agricultural labor. Copies of this bibliography are available from the Institute of Industrial Relations, University of California, Los Angeles.

For many phases of the farm labor movement, however, the reader is still largely on his own. He must delve here and there, in magazines, newspapers, legislative hearings, and try to put the bits and pieces together. There is, to this day, no really satisfactory, comprehensive, published account of the wetback traffic; the bracero program; the use of prisoners, foreign and domestic, in California agriculture; the period of "revolutionary unionism"; the Agricultural Workers Organizing Committee; and many other important chapters of the total saga. We have tried to tell them here, as space has permitted, but the fields and orchards are still broad and open and only partially charted.

Index

Index